INDIANA CABINETS

with Prices

L-W BOOK SALES

P.O. Box 69

Gas City, IN 46933

ISBN#0-89538-094-3

Published by: L-W Book Sales
                P.O. Box 69
                Gas City, IN 46933

Please write our company for a free catalog

Table of Contents

Pricing Information

All cabinets priced are in refinished condition. A cabinet in mint condition (original paint <u>perfect</u> – no chips, stains, etc.) will bring more.

The values in this book should be used only as a guide. These prices will vary from one section of the country to the other. All prices are also affected by the condition as well as the demand of the piece.

Neither the Author nor the Publisher assumes responsibility for any gains or losses that might be incurred as a result of using this guide.

Introduction

Early 20th Century kitchen cabinets and furnishings are not the typical antique or collectible as compared to the usual types of items which gather at auctions, antique shows, dealer shops, and the like. Emerging from a simpler time when employed craftsmen took pride in their meticulous work, these kitchen cabinets from the Hoosier heartland not only remind us of these times in their strength and beauty – they still maintain the function for which they were built.

Ordinary day-to-day usage should provide little threat to these monuments, although the attrition they suffer as the decades pass may present a problem. Wormholes, termite infestation, gradual warping due to humidity fluctuation, and other factors may contribute to the necessity of restoration of an aged kitchen cabinet. It is for this reason that the values determined within these pages are intended for those cabinets which have had some amount of restoration done.

It is also understood that, although there are exceptions to be found, old kitchen cabinets are usually found isolated within a home setting, rather than one item amongst many within an individual's collection. Regarding this matter, although many enthusiasts have a deep interest of antique furniture and furnishings, a person should consider themselves fortunate to actually have one within their possession. The kitchen cabinet's utilitarian usage provides as much worth in its purpose as it does for any aesthetic reason. Remember, years ago when they were being constructed and marketed, these cabinets were often included as the main part of an entire kitchen setting offered by the manufacturer.

Acknowledgments

L-W Books would like to thank Carol Ellis of Canton, Illinois, for the pictures of her Hoosier Cabinets. She is a real great friend, and we appreciate her very much. Thanks Carol!!!!

L-W Book Publishing would like to extend their gratitude to Mr. Allen Hyatt, who generously took the time out of his own schedule in order to set the pricing for the cabinets depicted within this guide. Allen continues the third generation of antique dealing within his family, specializing in antique furniture, especially kitchen furnishings and cabinets of this sort. He has spent the last ten years full time dealing with his interests, spending all his time in antique shops, shows, and auctions. Although refinishing and restoration are among his many talents, he does not participate in refinishing as a business, instead working on old cabinets with the intention to sell. Indiana cabinet enthusiasts can contact Mr. Allen Hyatt as follows by phone or email: ahyatt@infocom.com

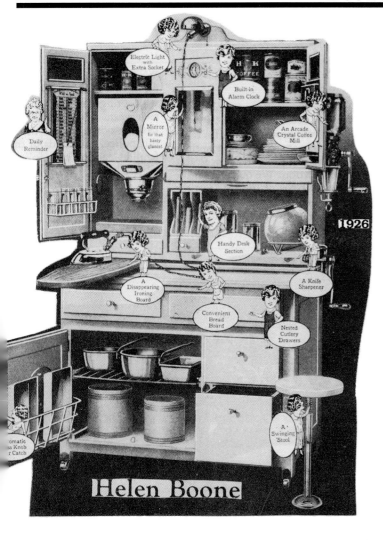

Helen Boone

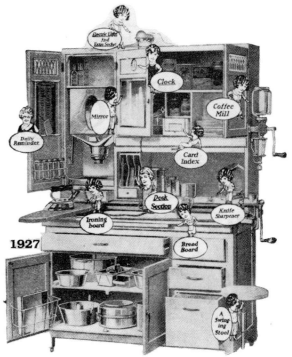

1927

Boone
DESIGNED BY 369 WOMEN

Baby Boone
for the kiddies

A miniature of Mary Boone, a substantial iron toy, white enamel, 8½ inches high. Doors that open and drawers that slide an' everything. Your youngster wants one "just like mother's". Sent for only $1.75 postpaid in U. S. A.

Dorothy Boone

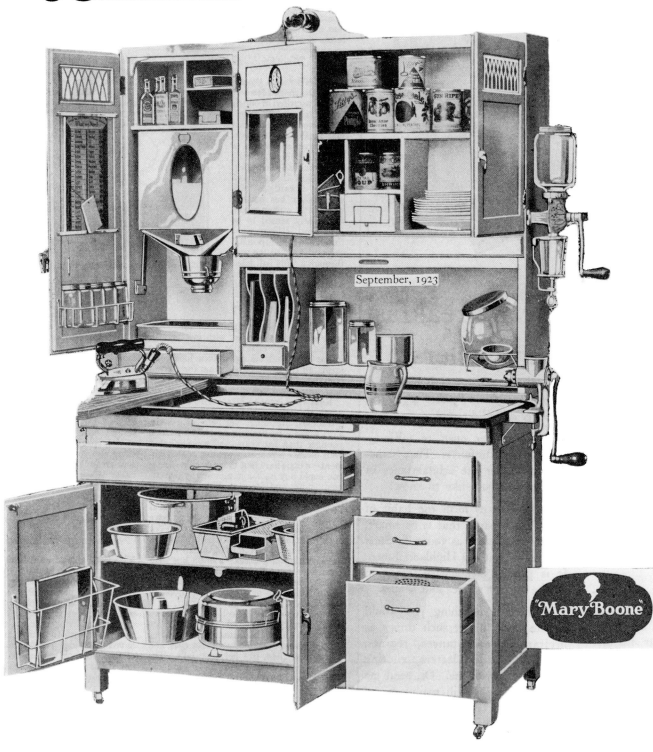

Hoosier Introduction

J.S. McQuinn and his son Emmett G. founded the Hoosier Manufacturing Company in 1899, in Albany, Indiana. Little more than a year had passed when the original factory caught fire and burned, so the Hoosier company soon resided in New Castle, located where the Speeder Bicycle Factory had previously been.

The Hoosier Manufacturing Company created new standards in the construction of kitchen cabinets. National advertising and sales worldwide manifested the Hoosier company as a household name. At the onset of the company, less than twenty employees crafted up to fifty and sixty portable kitchen cabinets each week. Eventually, at its peak the company employed well over seven hundred workers, alongside fifty or so traveling salesmen and an office crew of another sixty or seventy.

A typical day consisted of shipping eight to ten train cars a day, with as many as eighty cabinets in any given load. These peaking years produced nearly seven hundred cabinets a day, each branded with the proud name "Hoosier Manufacturing Company".

At this time the Hoosier company was the largest manufacturer of kitchen cabinets in America. Yet, with the introduction of the more popular built-in cabinets, the demand for portable kitchen cabinets plummeted. During the last few years of operation, the majority of output by the company was unit after unit of built-in cabinets and breakfast sets. In 1942, the Hoosier Manufacturing Company closed its doors one final time.

According to the late James S. McQuinn, the company originated when three others and himself formed a scheme to gain ownership of a furniture factory no longer in use in Albany, Indiana. These entrepreneurs included McQuinn himself, his son Emmett G. McQuinn, T. F. Hart, and J. M. Maring, although the McQuinn's were designated as active managers. After the passing of James S. McQuinn in November of 1938, E. G. McQuinn then became president of the company.

Although the company was plagued by problems in its formative years, proper management led the organization through these tough times. In order to help relieve the slow business during the summer season, they produced and sold a new patented seed separator. The seed separator did not revive the business as they had planned, yet combining sales pitches by offering the kitchen cabinets as an "alternative" for the farmer's wife if they were disinterested in the seed separator, this sales force proved successful. Before long, the Hoosier seed separator became a thing of the past and the company decided from that point on to concentrate on kitchen furniture. Although at first the kitchen cabinet seemed to most potential customers as a unneeded luxury, dealers were finally satisfied when a host of national advertising paved an easier route through the questionable attitudes of these conservative customers. The proclamation of a factory direct sales pitch inspired dealer and customer alike to become interested once and for all.

The Hoosier Manufacturing Company was the first major business to implement the "dollar down, dollar-a-week" policy, with many firms and businesses following suit with this successful idea. At this point, every town in the United States had an agency selling Hoosier cabinets, and many foreign countries had similar agencies as well.

Before much time had passed, wall cabinets and built-in units had become the most popular of kitchen equipment. The Hoosier company soon began the manufacture of these sorts of furnishings.

These built-in Hoosier cabinets extended further the grand reputation of the Hoosier company, and soon these cabinets were found in private homes and huge apartment house developments in major cities throughout the country.

By the 1940s, steel cabinets had become the popular option for customers – yet unfortunately, wartime rationing had begun once again and metal was in short supply. Due to severely increased costs for materials and labor, the Hoosier Kitchen Cabinet Factory was sold in 1942.

The Hoosier cabinet was the first cabinet designed and implemented to serve many functions for the "modern" homemaker. All the supplies and materials needed to complete a family luncheon was organized within hand's reach. The kitchen cabinets evolved slowly at first, when the drawers and holding cabinets for foodstuffs and utensils were oriented underneath the table top. Within a few design changes, everything except for the icebox was contained therein, eliminating the necessity of the pantry and cellar. Just as the advertising slogans boasted, it was a "step-saving and labor-saving device". The illustrated seventeen-step demonstration manual provided a close glimpse at the best of the features of the cabinets. The flour sifter and bin located in the top of the cabinet benefited greatly from the airtight construction and noncorrosive metal components, added to the convenience that it held up to 65 pounds of flour. The installation of a "tilt-jar" for sugar provided another gleam in the eyes of customers, alongside nearby placement of containers for spices, coffee, and tea. The large work-top surface, which could be further enlarged by means of a pullout shelf, made possible a number of tasks there at the homemaker's station, including such necessary chores as baking, ironing, and mending. The surface of the work-top was usually composed of aluminum or porcelain-enameled steel. Along with other features such as sectioned utensil drawers, a metal bread drawer, hanging racks for pots, and ball-bearing casters, how could a responsible housewife say no?

The Hoosier cabinets were advertised as "to last a lifetime" – and fortunately for enthusiasts such as ourselves, they have survived.

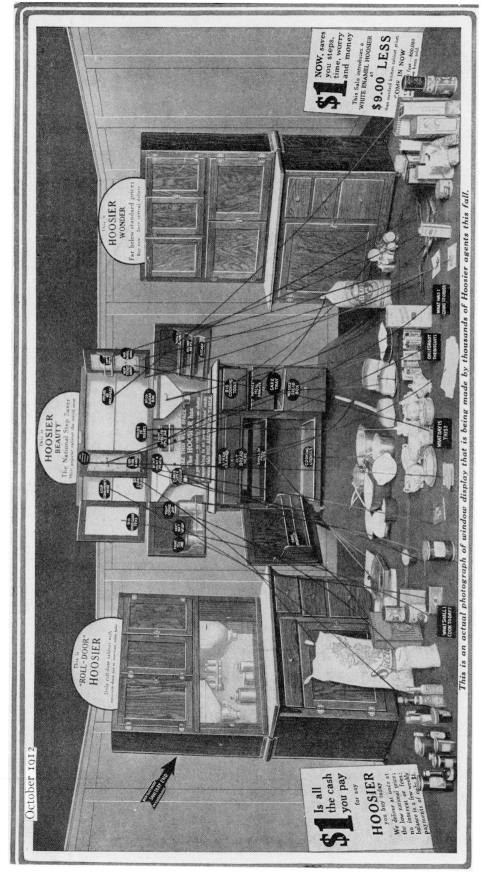

A catalog page from October 1912

The Hoosier Manufacturing Company was the first to use the "$1 down, $1 a week policy." This ingenious sales plan alone boosted sales and employment. At this time hundreds of agents were employed throughout the country to advertise this policy.

1907

Originators and pioneer makers of Kitchen Cabinets

No. 41—Price, $7.95

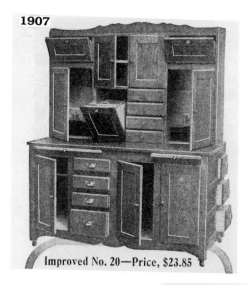

1907

Improved No. 20—Price, $23.85

1906

Household Economy

is as much a matter of saving your steps as of thrifty living. There is more time and strength left for other things if you have a

Hoosier Kitchen Cabinet

Convenient, compact, orderly. Everything a cook needs is at her fingers' ends. This No. 20 is often used instead of a "built in" cupboard. Can be put where you wish. Made of hard wood, best finish. Other cabinets, sewing tables, etc., $5.50 and up. Write for catalogue, free.

This trade mark is on every Cabinet—Don't buy until you see our catalog or a real "Hoosier" Cabinet.

THE HOOSIER MFG. CO., 14 Adams St., New Castle, Ind.

1909

Flour Bin

The flour is put in at the top, passes through the entire bin, and is taken out thoroughly sifted at the bottom. Thus no mouldy flour can accumulate. The bin is self-cleaning, made of metal and white wood.

Recipe Cabinet

100 recipe cards, labelled Bread, Cake and Desserts, Eggs, Fish, Meats, Miscellaneous, Salads, Sauces, Soups, Vegetables.

Spice Cabinet

contains six air-tight cans, highly finished and labelled Ginger, Cloves, Cream of Tartar, Allspice, Baking Powder and Cinnamon.

Sugar Bin

The sugar bin is the most cleverly devised bin in the Hoosier. The bulk of the sugar is held in the upper part of the bin as the opening is only large enough to allow a small quantity to run in the lower part. When a scoopful is taken out the same quantity drops down.

Aluminum Work-Table Top

can be drawn out beyond the front of the cabinet over 11 inches, adding more than one-third to the working space.

Want List

Everything needed in the kitchen, alphabetically arranged — simple and effective system for keeping stock.

These are some of the earlier Hoosier cabinets manufactured in the early 1900s.

1905

Cabinet No. 141, circa 1905

Equipped with an aluminum covered pull out table top, this Hoosier cabinet was dated circa 1910. The cabinet included six doors and three drawers, with a built in spice rack and clear glass doors for displaying your china.

This is possibly a variation of Cabinet No. 162, circa 1910

Equipped with an aluminum covered pull out table top, this Hoosier cabinet was dated circa 1905. Included with the cabinet were spice cans, coffee and tea canisters. The bottom featured metal racks for pie pans and other utensils and a sliding shelf for pots and pans to be stored on.

1910

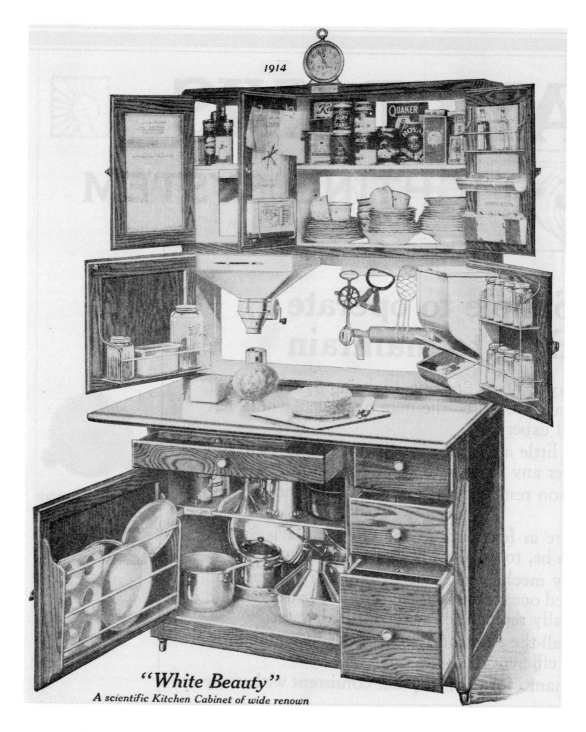

1914

"White Beauty"
A scientific Kitchen Cabinet of wide renown

The "White Beauty", circa 1914, was made of white enamel with either hinge or roll doors. The size was the same as any other "Hoosier Beauty" lines.

Height - 71 1/4"

Width - 41"

Hoosier

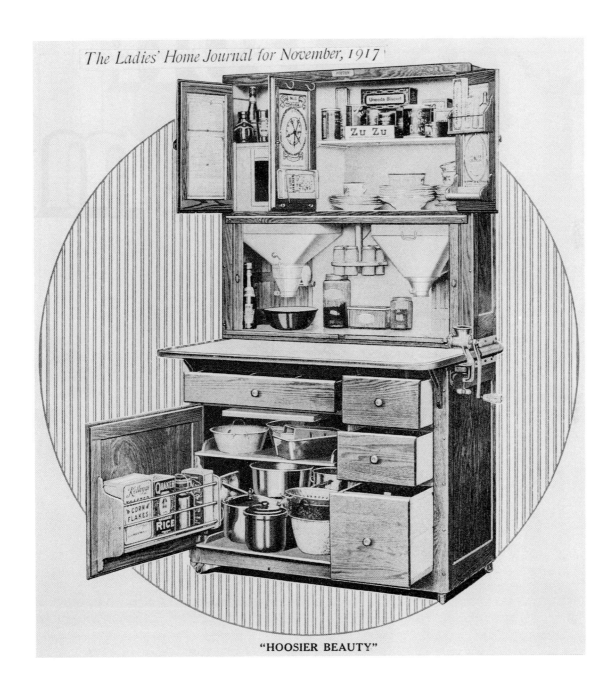

The Ladies' Home Journal for November, 1917

"HOOSIER BEAUTY"

The Hoosier "Beauty" was probably the most popular Hoosier cabinet made. It was said that of all the Hoosier cabinets purchased, 80% of them were the "Hoosier Beauty" models. There were three variations of the "Beauty", the first being the color or material used either oak or white enameled. The second was the doors, you had your choice of roll or hinge doors. The third and more evident in later years was the number of cutlery drawers.

This Hoosier "Beauty" had the roll doors and had a height of 71 1/2" and a width of 41".

The Hoosier cabinets described on this page were individual units custom made for the consumers kitchen and work space that was available.

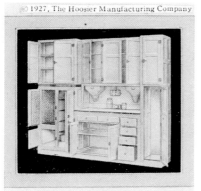

The concentration of kitchen needs so efficiently provided in this unit will save you thousands of steps

A compact combination of Hoosier Units including a working table, refrigerator, and an amazing amount of shelf, drawer and closet space

The Hoosier cabinets shown in this middle picture were made for apartments and small kitchens that were in need of any extra space that could be obtained

Another Hoosier unit showing the variation in style that enables you to find a Hoosier kitchen for any type of home

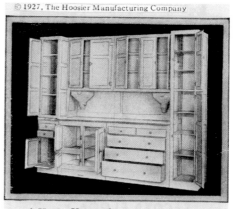

A Hoosier Unit combination containing a generous working table, shelves, drawers and closets to delight any woman's heart

A page from the Hoosier Cabinet Book "You and Your Kitchen", copyright 1914

Hoosier Cabinet No. 1429
The Famous "White Beauty"
Queen of the Line

Hoosier Cabinet No. 1429

Below is complete list of equipment you get with at no extra charge. Equipment in this cabinet not included in the preceding cabinets is described in italics.

New Features Shown for the First Time in a Hoosier Cabinet

Upper Section

Mrs. Christine Frederick's Housekeepers' Food Guide, showing an unlimited number of balanced menus (upper left door).

Bill file for meat and grocery bills (upper middle door).

Cook-book holder, for open or closed book (upper middle door).

Labeled compartment tray for milk tickets, money, etc. (upper right door).

Labeled hooks for can opener, ice book and milk bottle opener (upper right door).

Favorite recipe metal card file and index, with convenient holder for any recipe while being used (upper right door).

Ten guide cards and fifty blanks for file.

Condiment cupboard over flour bin.

Pencil holder on flour bin.

Lower Section

Cutlery drawer with three compartments (under table).

Special compartment for string in cutlery drawer.

Metal drawer under table for storing cereals and pastry flour.

Metal drawer for kitchen linen (above bread box).

Sliding shelf with asbestos bottom for storing iced cake or pastry in bread box.

Canned goods shelf—capacity five jars (in pot cupboard).

Standard Features that Have Made the Hoosier Famous

Upper Section

Sanitary, self-cleaning, metal flour bin; 50 pounds capacity.

Pantry shelf that holds 40 or more cereals and packages.

Roomy cupboard that holds 70 or more dishes.

Sanitary rolling pin rack.

Handy utensil hooks.

Clock-faced, patented want list (upper middle door).

Flavoring extract shelf (upper right door).

Crystal glass tea and coffee jars with air-tight screw lids (lower left door).

Crystal glass salt jar (lower left door).

Eight crystal glass spice jars, air-tight screw lids (lower right door).

Self-feeding metal sugar bin with dust-proof lids (lower right door).

Metal sugar scoop (in sugar bin).

Lower Section

Full extension, patented metal table, 42 x 39"—larger, more convenient than a kitchen table—slides out 16" beyond the base.

Convenient cutting board under table.

Metal, mouse-proof bread and cake box, self-closing lid (lower drawer).

Large pot and kettle cupboard.

Sliding shelf for pots and pans.

Pocket for pans and lid on pot cupboard door.

Construction

Light, Golden Oak outside finish, water and steam proof.

Ball-bearing casters of high-grade pressed steel.

Nickel-plated door fasteners.

Nickel-plated outside hinges.

Ivory-white inside finish, upper section.

Doors and wood drawer varnished inside.

Size

Height, 71"—width, 42"—depth of table, closed, 28"; open, 39".

Hoosier

A page from the Hoosier Cabinet Book "You and Your Kitchen", copyright 1914

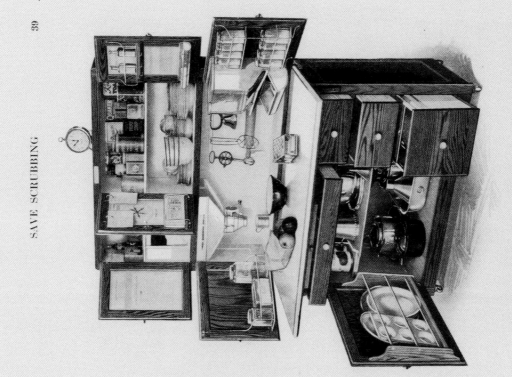

SAVE SCRUBBING

Hoosier Cabinet No. 1428

A Good Cabinet With White Cupboards

HOOSIER CABINETS

Hoosier Cabinet No. 1428

Below is complete list of equipment you get with it at no extra charge. Equipment in this cabinet not included in the preceding cabinets is described in italics.

New Features Shown for the First Time in a Hoosier Cabinet

Upper Section

Mrs. Christine Frederick's House-keepers' Food Guide, showing an unlimited number of balanced menus (upper left door).

Bill file for meat and grocery bills (upper middle door).

Cook-book holder, for open or closed book (upper middle door).

Labeled compartment tray for milk tickets, money, etc. (upper right door).

Labeled hooks for can opener, ice book and milk bottle opener (upper right door).

Condiment cupboard, over flour bin.

Pencil holder on flour bin.

Patented, sanitary, shaker flour sifter that shakes flour through instead of grinding it through (four times as fast as old style sifter, and can never wear out).

Lower Section

Cutlery drawer with three compart-ments (under table).

Special compartment for string in cutlery drawer.

Sliding metal shelf with asbestos bottom for storing iced cake or pastry in bread box.

Canned goods shelf—capacity, five jars (in pot cupboard).

Standard Features that Have Made the Hoosier Famous

Upper Section

Sanitary, self-cleaning, metal flour bin; 50 pounds capacity.

Pantry shelf that holds 40 or more cereals and packages.

Roomy cupboard that holds 70 or more dishes.

Sanitary rolling pin rack.

Handy utensil hooks.

Clock-faced, patented want list (upper middle door).

Flavoring extract shelf (upper right door).

Crystal glass tea and coffee jars with air-tight screw lids (lower left door).

Crystal glass salt jar (lower left door).

Eight crystal glass spice jars, air-tight screw lids (lower right door).

Self-feeding metal sugar bin with dust-proof lids (lower right door).

Metal sugar scoop (in sugar bin).

Lower Section

Full extension, patented metal table, 42 x 39″—larger, more convenient than a kitchen table—slides out 16″ beyond the base.

Convenient cutting board under table.

Drawer under table for storing cereals and pastry flour.

Drawer for kitchen linen (above bread box).

Metal, mouse-proof bread and cake box, self-closing lid (lower drawer in base).

Large pot and kettle cupboard.

Sliding shelf for pots and pans.

Pocket for pans and lids on pot cup-board door.

Construction

Light, Golden Oak outside finish, water and steam proof.

Ball-bearing casters of high-grade pressed steel.

Nickel-plated door fasteners.

Nickel-plated outside hinges.

Ivory-white inside finish, upper section.

Size

Height, 71″; width, 42″; depth of table, closed, 28½″; open, 39½″.

Hoosier

A page from the Hoosier Cabinet Book "You and Your Kitchen", copyright 1915

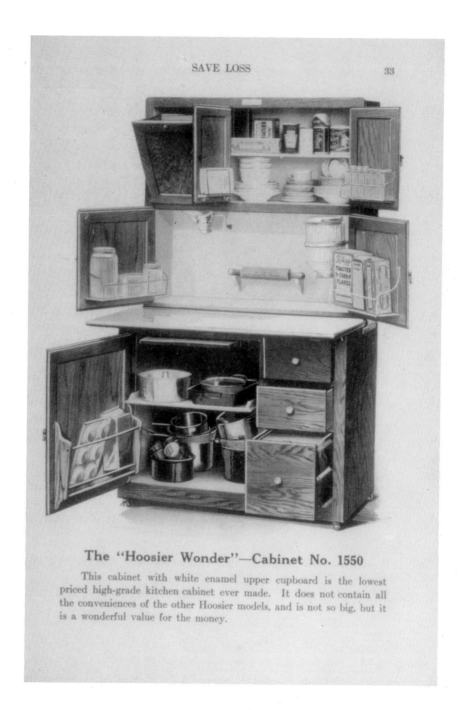

SAVE LOSS   33

The "Hoosier Wonder"—Cabinet No. 1550

This cabinet with white enamel upper cupboard is the lowest priced high-grade kitchen cabinet ever made. It does not contain all the conveniences of the other Hoosier models, and is not so big, but it is a wonderful value for the money.

Hoosier

A page from the Hoosier Cabinet Book "You and Your Kitchen", copyright 1915

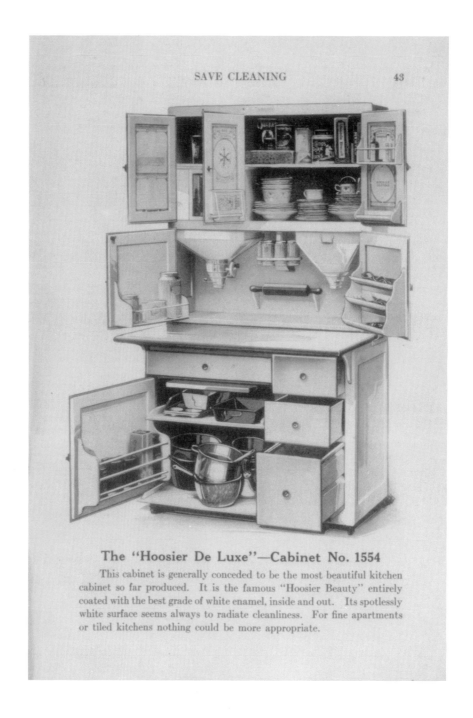

SAVE CLEANING   43

The "Hoosier De Luxe"—Cabinet No. 1554

This cabinet is generally conceded to be the most beautiful kitchen cabinet so far produced. It is the famous "Hoosier Beauty" entirely coated with the best grade of white enamel, inside and out. Its spotlessly white surface seems always to radiate cleanliness. For fine apartments or tiled kitchens nothing could be more appropriate.

A page from the Hoosier Cabinet Book "New Kitchen Short Cuts", copyright 1917

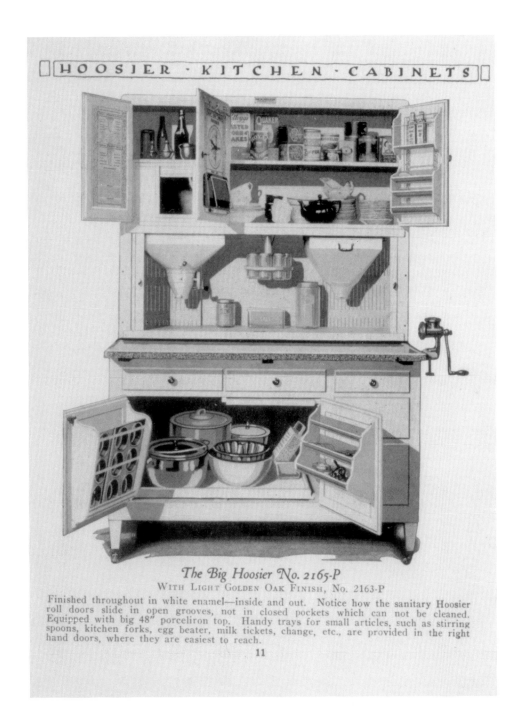

The Big Hoosier No. 2165-P
WITH LIGHT GOLDEN OAK FINISH, No. 2163-P

Finished throughout in white enamel—inside and out. Notice how the sanitary Hoosier roll doors slide in open grooves, not in closed pockets which can not be cleaned. Equipped with big 48″ porceliron top. Handy trays for small articles, such as stirring spoons, kitchen forks, egg beater, milk tickets, change, etc., are provided in the right hand doors, where they are easiest to reach.

11

Hoosier

A page from the Hoosier Cabinet Book "New Kitchen Short Cuts", copyright 1917

HOOSIER · KITCHEN · CABINETS

Hoosier Standard No. 2143-P

WITH PORCELIRON TABLE
WITH ALUMINUM TABLE, No. 2143
A very good Hoosier, convenient and durable.

15

The Hollenbeck Press Indianapolis

THIRTY-SIX-INCH HOOSIER

Size, 37″ wide, 71½″ high; Work Space, 34½ x 36″

No. 2337P—WHITE ENAMEL, as illustrated. Also made in LIGHT GOLDEN OAK—No. 2335P

Equipment includes white Porceliron top, 24 x 36 inches; mouse-proof construction; ant-proof casters; shaker flour sifter; 9-piece glassware set; package rack on lower door; shallow utensil tray suspended from work-table, etc.

This Hoosier "Special" circa 1912 with its see through china cupboard, aluminum covered work table and sanitary flour bin was a very popular model, second only to the "Hoosier Beauty".

Height:	70 1/4 inches
Width:	40 inches
Lower Section:	28 inches
Table Space:	40 x 39 inches

January, 1925

September 15, 1928

Top Photo

The 48" wide Hoosier "Highboy" came standard with a porcelain top, ant-proof casters, and a 14 piece glassware set.

Bottom Photo

The 42" wide Hoosier "Highboy" came standard with a porcelain top, and ant-proof casters. This highboy style and dimensions are the same as the Hoosier "Beauty" except for the height, which the Highboy is 10 1/2" taller.

December, 1925

This is a 41" wide Hoosier "Highboy". Though the widths of the Highboy changed through the years, the height stayed relatively the same at 82". With this in mind, it is an easy way to identify a "Highboy" Hoosier cabinet.

THE HOOSIER HIGHBOY—*41-inch Model*

Extreme width of cabinet	41 inches	Depth of base section	21¾ inches
Width of extension work table	40½ inches	Depth of work table (closed)	27 inches
Depth of upper section	13 inches	Depth of work table (extended)	36 inches

Height (When equipped with standard 5-inch legs) 82 inches

Light Golden Oak—No. 2577-GO.   White Enamel—No. 2577-WE.   French Grey—No. 2577-FG.

1925

TILTING-BIN HOOSIER

EQUIPMENT includes: white porceliron or aluminum work table, 25 x 40½ inches; ant-proof casters; 6-piece glassware set; glass sugar bowl; lower drawer of metal.

Width, 41 inches; height, 70 inches; work space, 34 x 40½.

Light Golden Oak—**No. 2520 A-GO** (aluminum)
White Enamel—**No. 2520 A-WE** (aluminum)
Light Golden Oak—**No. 2520-GO** (porceliron)
White Enamel—**No. 2520-WE** (porceliron)

1925

ACCESSORIES FOR YOUR HOOSIER CABINETS.

THE HOOSIER WORK TABLE

THERE are so many times when, no matter how much work space there is in the kitchen, it never seems enough. At such times this work table has a special value as a supplement to the Hoosier cabinet. It has three roomy drawers and a handy cutting board; is finished to match the other Hoosier furniture—in White or French Grey enamel with blue decoration, porceliron top and nickel drawer pulls. In two sizes:

White Enamel, **No. 11-WE**; French Grey, **No. 11-FG**; 25 x 40½ inches.
White Enamel, **No. 14-WE**; French Grey, **No. 14-FG**; 27 x 48 inches.

1925

HOOSIER BREAKFAST SET
—CHARMING, PRACTICAL, INEXPENSIVE!

DAINTY enough to appeal to any woman—and strong enough to meet her most exacting needs. The neat blue decoration gives a touch of color that makes the set an attractive addition to the kitchen.

For a cozy breakfast nook; for the "rest corner" of your kitchen; and to supplement your Hoosier cabinet when canning or serving company—this set is invaluable.

The tables, in three sizes; also the chairs, with strong double cane seats and backs low enough to slide under the edge of the table, may be bought separately at surprisingly small cost, either White Enamel (WE) or French Grey (FG).

All tables are 30 inches high, are equipped with porceliron tops, heavy metal corner clamps, nickel drawer pulls and metal slides.

White Enamel, No. 0-WE; French Grey, No. 0-FG; 24 x 36 inches, not decorated.
White Enamel, No. 1-WE; French Grey, No. 1-FG; 25 x 40½ inches, decorated.
White Enamel, No. 4-WE; French Grey, No. 4-FG; 27 x 48 inches, decorated.

1925

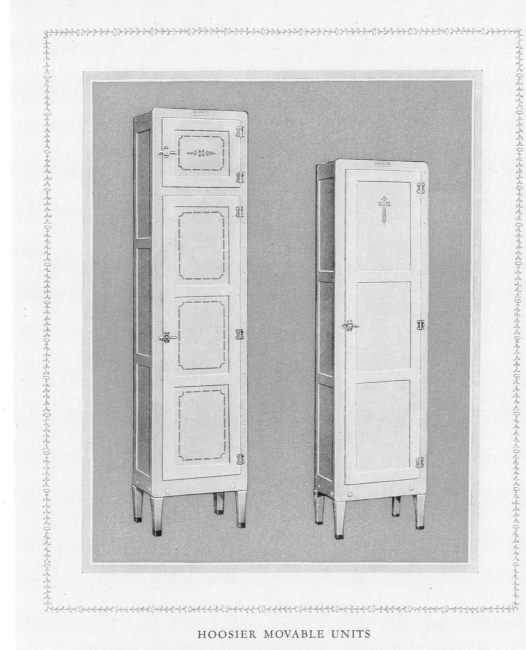

HOOSIER MOVABLE UNITS

EQUIPPED as storage cupboards or as broom closets, are available in two heights and three finishes corresponding to Hoosier Highboy and Hoosier Beauty Cabinets.

See pages 22 and 23 for further description.

All unit doors are hinged on right side unless otherwise specified.

1925

HOOSIER MOVABLE UNITS (HIGHBOY HEIGHT)

SHELF UNIT, equipped with five wide, adjustable shelves and racks as shown, for storage of dishes, supplies and utensils. Broom Unit, equipped with four narrow shelves, broom clips and racks for brooms, vacuum and all cleaning-day necessities.

Height, 82 inches; depth, 13 inches; width, 20¼ inches

HOOSIER SHELF UNIT	HOOSIER BROOM UNIT
Light Golden Oak—No. 5212-GO.	Light Golden Oak—No. 5211-GO.
White Enamel—No. 5212-WE.	White Enamel—No. 5211-WE.
French Grey—No. 5212-FG.	French Grey—No. 5211-FG.

1925

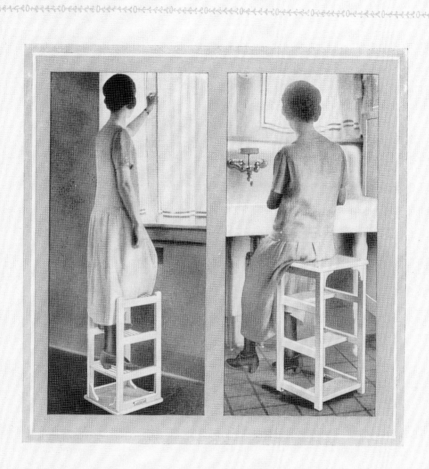

THE HOOSIER COMBINATION STOOL AND STEP-LADDER

ONE of the handiest little pieces of Hoosier equipment is this combination stool and step-ladder. A stool of more than chair seat height is always a convenience at the sink or cabinet. And where is the house that doesn't need a low, light step-ladder? All you need to do is to reverse the stool and you have your steps, covered with rubber mats to prevent slipping.

Oak—**No. 51-GO.** White Enamel—**No. 51-WE.**
French Grey—**No. 51-FG.**

1925

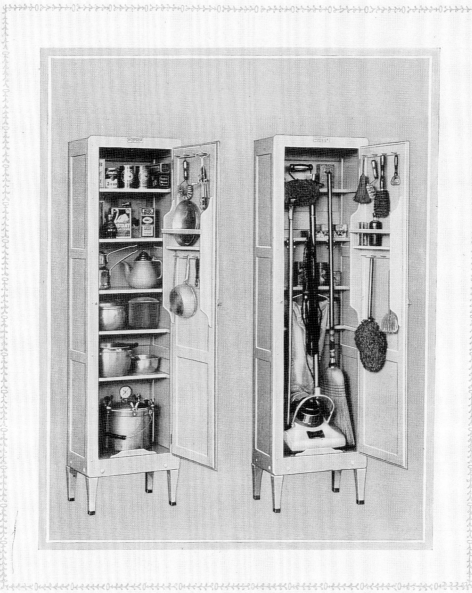

HOOSIER MOVABLE UNITS (BEAUTY HEIGHT)

SHELF UNIT, equipped with five wide, adjustable shelves and rack as shown, for storage of dishes, supplies and utensils. Broom Unit, equipped with four narrow shelves, broom clips, rack and hooks, for brooms, vacuum and all cleaning-day necessities.

Height, 72 inches; depth, 13 inches; width, 20¼ inches.

HOOSIER SHELF UNIT	HOOSIER BROOM UNIT
Light Golden Oak—No. 5002-GO.	Light Golden Oak—No. 5001-GO.
White Enamel—No. 5002-WE.	White Enamel—No. 5001-WE.
French Grey—No. 5002-FG.	French Grey—No. 5001-FG.

1925

A page from the Hoosier Cabinet Book "You and Your Kitchen", copyright 1914

SAVE DUSTING

37

Hoosier Cabinet No. 1427
A Popular Model

36   HOOSIER CABINETS

Hoosier Cabinet No. 1427

Below is complete list of equipment you get with it at no extra charge. Equipment in this cabinet not included in the preceding cabinets is described in italics.

New Features Shown for the First Time in a Hoosier Cabinet

Upper Section

Mrs. Christine Frederick's House-keepers' Food Guide, showing an unlimited number of balanced menus (upper left door).

Bill file for meat and grocery bills, (upper middle door).

Cook-book holder, for open or closed book (upper middle door).

Labeled compartment tray for milk tickets, money, etc. (upper right door).

Labeled hooks for can opener, ice book, and milk bottle opener (upper right door).

Condiment cupboard, over flour bin.

Pencil holder on flour bin.

Lower Section

Cutlery drawer with three compartments (under table).

Special compartment for string in cutlery drawer.

Sliding metal shelf with asbestos bottom for storing iced cake or pastry in bread box.

Canned goods shelf—capacity five jars (in pot cupboard).

Standard Features that Have Made the Hoosier Famous

Upper Section

Sanitary, self-cleaning, metal flour bin; 50 pounds capacity.

Pantry shelf that holds 40 or more cereals and packages.

Roomy cupboard that holds 70 or more dishes.

Sanitary rolling pin rack.

Handy utensil hooks.

Clock-faced, patented want list (upper middle door).

Flavoring extract shelf (upper right door).

Crystal glass tea and coffee jars with air-tight screw lids (lower left door).

Crystal glass salt jar (lower left door).

Eight crystal glass spice jars, air-tight screw lids (lower right door).

Self-feeding metal sugar bin with dust-proof lids (lower right door).

Metal sugar scoop (in sugar bin).

Lower Section

Full extension, patented metal table, 42 x 39″—larger, more convenient than a kitchen table—slides out 16″ beyond the base.

Convenient cutting board under table.

Drawer under table for storing cereals and pastry flour.

Drawer for kitchen linen (above bread box).

Metal, mouse-proof bread and cake box, self-closing lid (lower drawer in base).

Large pot and kettle cupboard.

Sliding shelf for pots and pans.

Pocket for pans and lids on pot cupboard door.

Construction

Light, Golden Oak outside finish, water and steam proof. *Oak back inside.*

Ball-bearing casters of high-grade pressed steel.

Nickel-plated door fasteners.

Nickel-plated outside hinges.

Size

Height, 71″—width, 42″—depth of table, closed, 28″; open, 39″.

A page from the Hoosier Cabinet Book "You and Your Kitchen", copyright 1914

Hoosier Cabinet No. 1425

This is a good cabinet slightly smaller than the other patterns. With white interior upper section, it is No. 1425½

Hoosier Cabinet No. 1425

Below is complete list of equipment you get with it at no extra charge. This Cabinet, with white interior upper section is No. 1425½.

It is 2 inches narrower than the other patterns.

New Features Shown for the First Time in a Hoosier Cabinet

Cook-book holder, for open or closed book (upper middle door).

Condiment cupboard, over flour bin.

Pencil holder on flour bin.

Standard Features that Have Made the Hoosier Famous

Upper Section

Sanitary, self-cleaning, metal flour bin; 50 pounds capacity.

Pantry shelf that holds 35 or more cereals and packages.

Roomy cupboard that holds 60 or more dishes.

Sanitary rolling pin rack.

Handy utensil hooks.

Clock-faced, patented want list (upper left door).

Flavoring extract shelf (upper right door).

Crystal glass tea and coffee jars with air-tight screw lids (lower left door).

Crystal glass salt jar (lower left door).

Six crystal glass spice jars, air-tight screw lids (lower right door).

Self-feeding metal sugar bin with dust-proof lids (lower right door).

Metal sugar scoop (in sugar bin).

Lower Section

Extension, patented metal table, 40x39"—larger, more convenient than a kitchen table—slides out 16" beyond the base.

Convenient cutting board under table.

Drawer under table at right side for cutlery.

Drawer for kitchen linen (above bread box).

Metal, mouse-proof bread and cake box, self-closing lid (lower drawer in base).

Large pot and kettle cupboard.

Sliding shelf for pots and pans.

Pocket for pans and lids on pot cupboard door.

Construction

Light, Golden Oak outside finish, water and steam proof.

Ball-bearing casters of high-grade pressed steel.

Nickel-plated door fasteners.

Nickel-plated outside hinges.

Size

Height, 71"—width, 40"—depth of table, closed, 28"; open, 39".

A page from the Hoosier Cabinet Book "You and Your Kitchen", copyright 1914

SAVE TOOLS

43

Hoosier Cabinet No. 1430

The New "Domestic Science School" Model

42

HOOSIER CABINETS

Hoosier Cabinet No. 1430

Below is complete list of equipment you get with it at no extra charge. Equipment in this cabinet not included in the preceding cabinets is described in italics.

New Features Shown for the First Time in a Hoosier Cabinet

Upper Section

Mrs. Christine Frederick's House-keepers' Food Guide, showing an unlimited number of balanced menus (upper left door).

Pencil holder on upper left door.

Bill file for meat and grocery bills (upper middle door).

Cook-book holder, for open or closed book (upper middle door).

Four crystal glass cruets, with glass stoppers, for flavoring extracts (upper right door).

Labeled hooks for ice book, milk bottle opener and can opener (upper right door).

Labeled compartment tray for milk tickets, money, etc. (upper right door).

Favorite recipe metal card file and index, with convenient holder for any recipe while being used (upper right door).

Ten guide cards and fifty blanks for file.

Condiment cupboard over flour bin.

Patented, sanitary shaker flour sifter that shakes flour through instead of grinding it through (four times as fast as an old style sifter and can never wear out).

Lower Section

Cutlery drawer with three compartments (under table).

Special compartment for string in cutlery drawer.

Metal drawer under table, for storing cereals and pastry flour.

Metal drawer for kitchen linen (above bread box).

Sliding shelf with asbestos bottom for storing iced cake or pastry in bread box.

Canned goods shelf—capacity five jars (in pot cupboard).

Standard Features that Have Made the Hoosier Famous

Upper Section

Sanitary, self-cleaning, metal flour bin; 50 pounds capacity.

Pantry that holds 40 or more cereals and packages.

Roomy cupboard that holds 70 or more dishes.

Handy utensil hooks.

Clock-faced, patented want list (upper middle door).

Flavoring extract shelf (upper right middle door).

Crystal glass tea and coffee jars with air-tight screw lids (upper left door).

Crystal glass salt jar.

Seven crystal glass jars, air-tight screw lids.

Self-cleaning, dust-proof metal sugar bin.

Metal sugar scoop (in sugar bin).

Revolving caster directly in front of table, on which are placed the glass spice jars, and below which is placed the salt jar.

Metal sugar bin with spout which fits a cup, equipped with cut-off valve.

Hard Rock Maple table, saturated with paraffine, absolutely waterproof and sanitary.

Lower Section

Convenient cutting board under table.

Metal, mouse-proof bread and cake box, self-closing lid (lower drawer).

Large pot and kettle cupboard.

Sliding shelf for pots and pans.

Pocket for pans and lids on pot cupboard door.

Construction

Light, Golden Oak outside finish, water and steam proof.

Ball-bearing casters of high-grade pressed steel.

Nickel-plated door fasteners.

Nickel-plated inside hinges.

Ivory-white inside finish, upper section.

Doors and wood drawer varnished inside.

Size

Height, 71''—width, 42''—depth of table, 38''.

THE HOOSIER HIGHBOY

Size, 42″ wide, 82″ high; Work Space, 37¼x41″

No. 2378P—White Enamel, as illustrated. Also made in Light Golden Oak—No. 2376P

ROLL DOOR HOOSIER BEAUTY

Size, 42" wide, 71½" high; Work Space, 37¼ x 41"

No. 2355P—White Enamel, as illustrated. Also made in Light Golden Oak—No. 2353P

Equipment includes white Porceliron top, 27 x 41 inches, operating on roller-spring tension; mouse-proof construction; ant-proof casters; shaker flour sifter; 14-piece glassware set; velvet-lined silverware extension drawer; extension cutlery drawer with compartments for 10-piece Domestic Science Cutlery Set, etc.

1927

THE 48-INCH HOOSIER HIGHBOY

Size, 49″ wide, 82″ high: Work Space, 37¼ x 48″

No. 2380P—WHITE ENAMEL, as illustrated. Also made in LIGHT GOLDEN OAK—No. 2379P

1927

HINGE DOOR HOOSIER BEAUTY

Size, 42″ wide, 71½″ high; Work Space, 37¼ x 41″

No. 2354P—WHITE ENAMEL, as illustrated. Also made in LIGHT GOLDEN OAK—**No. 2352P**

Equipment includes white Porceliron top, 27 x 41 inches, operating on roller-spring tension; mouse-proof construction; ant-proof casters; shaker flour sifter; 14-piece glassware set; velvet-lined silverware extension drawer; extension cutlery drawer with compartments for 10-piece Domestic Science Cutlery Set, etc.

1927

The Hoosier Special Closed
This is how your cabinet will look when you first see it

1925

HOOSIER SPECIAL

Size, 42″ wide, 71½″ high; Work Space, 35¼ x 40½″

No. 2345P—White Enamel, as illustrated. Also made in Light Golden Oak—No. 2343P

Equipment includes white Porceliron top, 25 x 40½ inches; ant-proof casters; shaker flour sifter; 10-piece glassware set; utensil racks on lower door, etc. Note—In this model only the lower drawer is made of metal.

1927

HOOSIER CABINET BASE

No. 234P—White Enamel
as illustrated

Also made in Light Golden
Oak—No. 233P

Equipment includes white Porceliron top, 27x41 inches, operating on roller-spring tension; mouse-proof construction; ant-proof casters; 14-piece crystal glassware set in addition to glass sugar bowl; velvet-lined silverware extension drawer; extension cutlery drawer with compartments for Domestic Science Cutlery Set, etc.

HOOSIER PORCELIRON TABLES

Table No. 0—24x36 inches, equipped with one-compartment drawer (19x20 inches).

Table No. 1—25x40½ inches, equipped with one-compartment drawer (19x20 inches).

Table No. 4—27x48 inches, equipped with 20x22½-inch drawer with three compartments.

All tables are 30 inches high. HOOSIER standard white enamel finish, and genuine white Porceliron tops. Nickel handles on drawers.

Tables are shipped knocked down, packed two of one size to a crate. Legs attach by means of convenient bolts.

F. 63-0, Printed in U.S.A., 4-23
By Bookwalter-Ball-Greathouse Ptg. Co.
Indianapolis, Ind.

1927

SPECIAL FEATURES FOR THE HOOSIER CABINETS

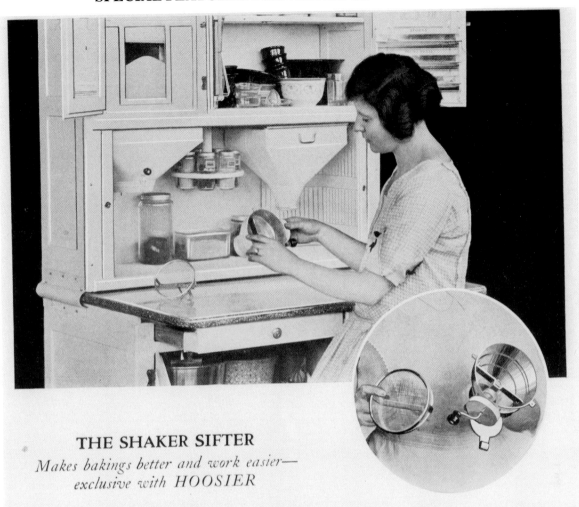

THE SHAKER SIFTER

Makes bakings better and work easier—
exclusive with HOOSIER

THE patented shaker flour sifter has long been an exclusive HOOSIER feature. Because it works four times as fast as other sifters, and fluffs the flour in addition to sifting it, this sifter actually enables HOOSIER owners to produce lighter and better breads, cakes and pastries.

In addition, the HOOSIER sifter keeps out all grit. By operating more swiftly and thoroughly, it saves work. One sifting is sufficient.

The special HOOSIER agitator insures that the flour will be fed into the sifter freely and evenly, even in damp weather.

The whole sifter is decidedly simple. It comes apart in an instant for cleaning. Because there is no wear on the sieving surface, there is no danger of broken sieve wires in food. The wire cup may be removed, and all parts are instantly accessible for cleaning.

1927

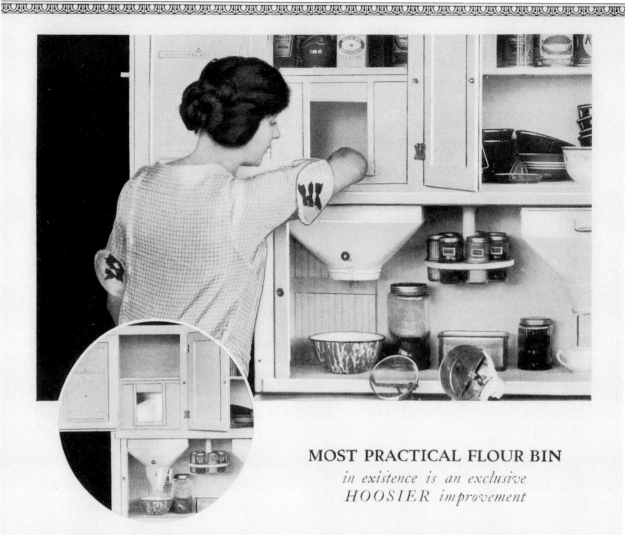

MOST PRACTICAL FLOUR BIN

in existence is an exclusive
HOOSIER improvement

EVERY type of flour bin that was ever invented has been tried out on the HOOSIER. The present bin was accepted as the best because it is the only bin that combines all these essential requirements: it has no mechanical features to get out of order; it is decidedly easy to fill; every part of the HOOSIER bin is easily accessible for cleaning; nothing but metal or glass touches the flour; since the oldest flour is always used first, the bin is practically self cleaning.

HOOSIER is the only cabinet in which it is easy to put flour back in the bin if more is sifted than is needed. It is the only cabinet with a sliding glass panel in the flour bin, which makes it easy to keep the bin sweet and clean.

A LOW Work Table for SHORT Women

A HIGH Work-Table for TALL Women

HOOSIER'S ADJUSTED HEIGHT

Prevents backaches and muscle strains

MUCH of the fatigue experienced by women is due to the strain of working at a table-top which is too high or too low. Unless kitchen work is placed at exactly the right height, such work as rolling dough, kneading bread, beating cakes, etc., is made much too difficult.

The HOOSIER is the only kitchen cabinet which makes it possible for every woman to have a work-table suited to her height.

This is done by means of detachable legs of different heights.

To secure a high table, long legs are inserted in the steel sockets. For a lower one, shorter legs are used. This is one of the most important improvements ever incorporated in a kitchen cabinet. It gives the HOOSIER the strongest leg construction of any cabinet in existence.

1927

REVOLVING SPICE CASTER

One of HOOSIER'S most noted exclusive conveniences

THE revolving spice caster is suspended directly above the table-top, just inside HOOSIER'S sanitary roll doors. Each spice is kept in a separate crystal glass container. Some of these containers are equipped with air-tight aluminum tops, others with perforated aluminum sifter tops, thus permitting the housewife to keep each seasoning in the handiest and most appropriate container. Printed labels are furnished so that the housewife may label the jars to show exactly the spice put in each one.

A single touch of the finger brings the exact spice desired directly to the hand.

Separate glass containers to be kept in the open cupboard which forms the back of the table space are provided for coffee, tea and salt. Still others for bulky foods—making a total of fourteen—are provided in the better cabinets in a compartment on the door to the lower section.

1927

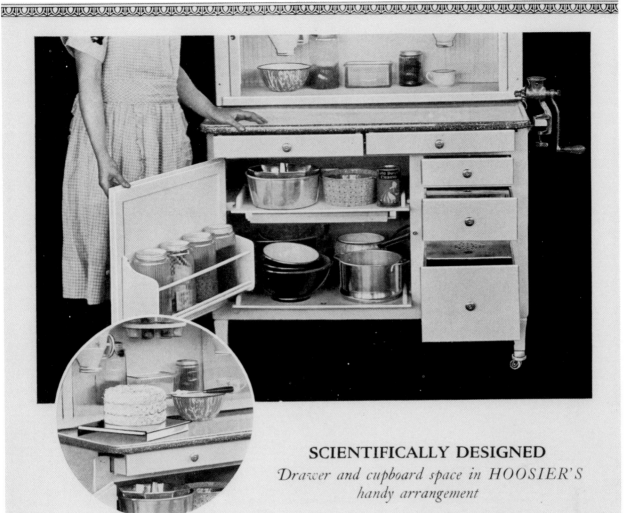

SCIENTIFICALLY DESIGNED

Drawer and cupboard space in HOOSIER'S handy arrangement

HOOSIER designers have provided unusually commodious drawer and cupboard capacity in the lower section of the cabinet—another feature that experience has proved necessary in a cabinet meant to give lasting satisfaction.

The two handy cutlery drawers slide backward and forward with the extension table-top. They are thus always in reach of the hand, even when the work-table is pulled all the way forward. The right-hand drawer is equipped with separate compartments for the Dexter Domestic Science Kitchen Set.

The two lower drawers are made of triple-plated metal, with ventilated lids of the same material, so that they may be used for foodstuffs if desired.

The lower drawer is the metal bread and cake box. It slides out on a support which keeps it from sagging even when it is loaded heavily.

This drawer is also equipped with a tray to be used in cooling or icing a cake. It is so made that a cake, when placed upon it, is cooled uniformly.

1927

FINISHED FRONT

*—and panelled ends, make HOOSIER
LAST LONGER*

THE upper section of the HOOSIER is finished with a frame put on with heavy screws that not only add attractiveness, but give longer life to the HOOSIER by making it more rigid.

This same type of frame construction is also used on the lower section.

The doors are attached to these casings and are thus made more secure and kept from drawing out of shape.

All panels in both upper and lower sections are three-ply. This type of construction takes care of any expansion and contraction which may come from varying kitchen temperature.

It also makes the cabinet more rigid, eliminates the danger of cracking and splitting, and keeps the cabinet from warping in kitchen steam.

HOOSIER'S years of experience in building a cabinet to withstand the steam and heat of the kitchen gives the assurance that the cabinet in service will be all it ought to be.

1927

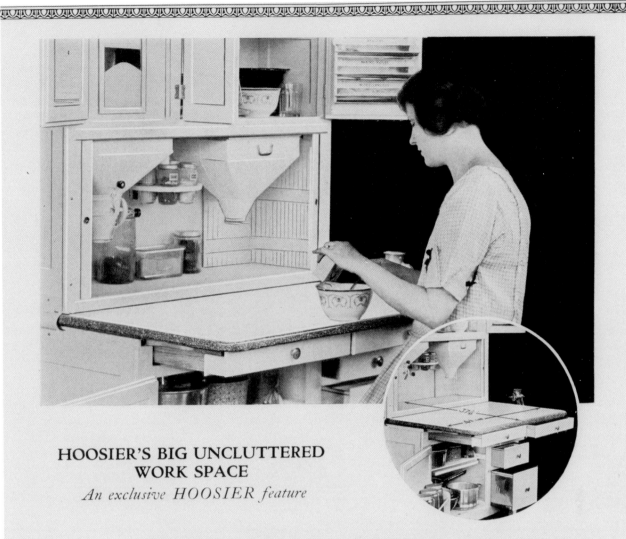

HOOSIER'S BIG UNCLUTTERED WORK SPACE

An exclusive HOOSIER feature

THE HOOSIER is the only kitchen cabinet which has a big uncluttered work space extending all the way across—all the way to the back of the cabinet—WITHOUT A SINGLE PARTITION OR OBSTRUCTION to get in the way or reduce the available working space. Because of this arrangement the housewife can always get her baking pans directly under the flour sifter, no matter how wide they may be.

Since ninety per cent. of all kitchen work is performed at this part of the cabinet, this unusually commodious table space is a decided HOOSIER advantage.

There is plenty of elbow room and a big enough table space to be of vital assistance in operations such as canning or getting a big meal, which always clutter up the old-fashioned type of kitchen and add to the work and worry.

1927

HOOSIER'S SUGAR BIN
Only one of its kind—and a fine HOOSIER improvement

THE HOOSIER metal sugar bin is another of the long-established, superior HOOSIER features that especially illustrates the care with which the HOOSIER is planned. Whereas, sugar bins in common use have a capacity of only seven or eight pounds, the HOOSIER bin takes care of a sufficient quantity to enable the owner to buy economically.

Furthermore, the HOOSIER sugar bin is the only bin from which it is equally convenient to scoop sugar from the top or draw it from the spout at the bottom. HOOSIER sugar bins are kept in place by a safety catch, can be quickly removed and are easily cleaned.

The sugar comes in contact only with the clean triple-plated metal.

1927

GLASS CONTAINERS

For bulk foods, a handy HOOSIER improvement

THE HOOSIER Beauty and Hoosier Highboy models are equipped with four air-tight crystal glass food containers with aluminum tops. These jars are large enough to carry a liberal supply of such bulk foods as beans, dried fruits, rice and hominy —in addition to the special provision made in the HOOSIER for flour, sugar, coffee, tea, salt and spices.

These crystal jars are placed on the lower door, where they are easiest to get at. They constitute a decided forward step in simplifying kitchen work by placing each thing in exactly the right place and thus saving time and steps.

The addition of these jars gives these HOOSIER patterns an equipment of fourteen pieces of crystal glassware.

1927

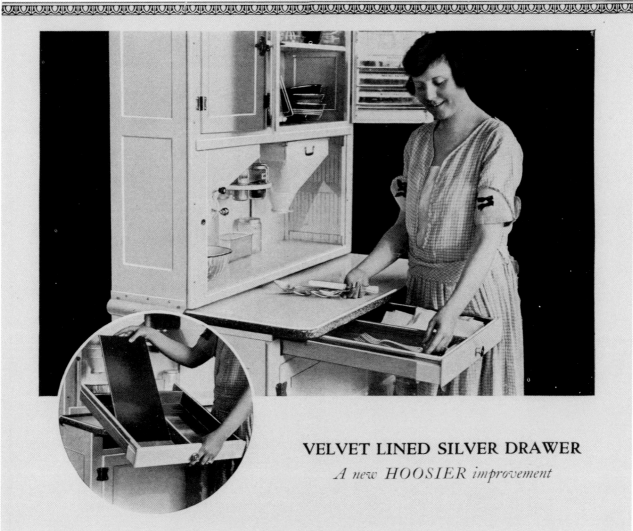

VELVET LINED SILVER DRAWER

A new HOOSIER improvement

FOR the convenience of the housewife who prefers to keep at least a portion of her table silver in the kitchen, the new HOOSIER provides a velvet-lined silverware compartment.

And this compartment is in the handiest place imaginable. It comprises one-half of a drawer which is suspended directly from the extending work-table. Even when the table is pulled its full length forward, this silver drawer and its contents are in easy reach of the hand.

A further convenience is found in the fact that the velvet pad in the bottom of the silver compartment is easily removed for brushing.

The other compartment in this extending drawer is a handy place to keep a working supply of fresh tea towels.

1927

HOOSIER CUTLERY DRAWER

*Makes it easy to find exactly the
right Knife, Fork or Spatula*

ONE of the special extension drawers suspended from the sliding work-table of the Hoosier Beauty, Highboy and Big Hoosier is especially fitted to accommodate the complete Dexter Domestic Science Kitchen Set.

This set consists of ten specialized kitchen tools, including strong pronged forks, paring knives, bread knives, meat knife, French trimming knife and two handy spatulas. This is the set which has been endorsed by many nationally famous domestic science experts. It is at its best in the special drawer provided for it in the HOOSIER.

Even when the work-table is extended the entire distance, this special drawer places the tool you want in direct reach of the hand. It is one of the most important HOOSIER improvements.

1927

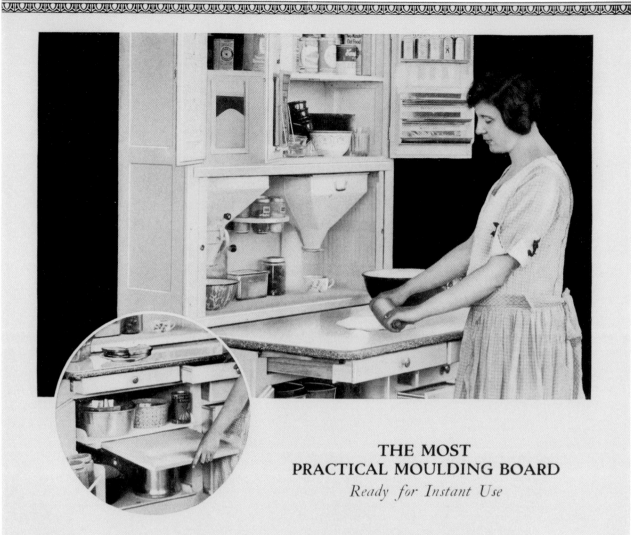

THE MOST
PRACTICAL MOULDING BOARD
Ready for Instant Use

HOOSIER'S gleaming white Porceliron top is the best moulding board in the world—and it is always in place, ready for instant use.

This clean, sanitary top, unlike a wooden board, has no pores for the dough to work into and turn sour. The dough will not stick on it, so that it is not necessary to use so much flour.

And since the work-table is held rigidly in place by special HOOSIER improvements there is no inconvenience from having the board shift about while being used.

In addition, HOOSIER provides a handy wooden cutting board, which slides into place below the shelf of the lower section. This board saves the Porceliron table-top and keeps the knives from being dulled. It is kept in a handy place, always easy to get at.

1927

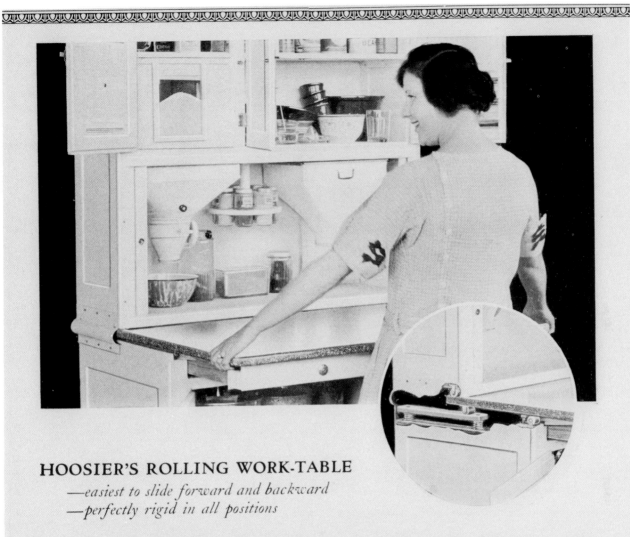

HOOSIER'S ROLLING WORK-TABLE

—easiest to slide forward and backward
—perfectly rigid in all positions

THE HOOSIER is the only cabinet with an extending work-table which slides backward and forward between roller bearings, operating under the easy, uniform pressure exerted by a tension-track supported by spiral springs.

Because of the rollers which are in constant contact with both the upper and under sides of the work-table, this table-top is surprisingly easy to operate.

And because of the tension supplied by the spring-track on which two of the rollers operate, the table is always rigid, even when but partly extended.

At all times, and in all positions, the work-table is absolutely free of all "rocking" or tilting. There is no play, either vertically or horizontally. Consequently, there is never any danger of food or utensils being knocked over by an inadvertent jar of the table.

This improvement is incorporated in the Beauty and High-boy models.

1927

MOUSE-PROOF, ANT-PROOF *and* DUST-PROOF CONSTRUCTION

Important to the Housewife

HOOSIER Beauty and Highboy cabinets are absolutely mouse-proof. The lower section is sealed against vermin and dust by means of a tightly-fitting top which gives the sharp teeth of rodents no opportunity to effect an entrance.

All cabinets in the HOOSIER line are protected against ants by means of metal ant cups just above the easy-rolling casters. By filling these cups with borax, tartar emetic, or a similar substance, the housewife can keep her cabinet free of ants.

With a similar view to absolute sanitation all doors are equipped with over-lapping dust strips.

These provisions make the HOOSIER the most sanitary cabinet in America.

1927

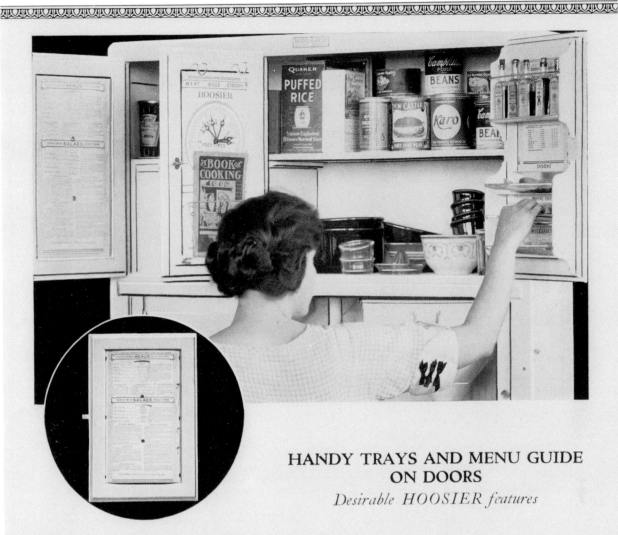

HANDY TRAYS AND MENU GUIDE ON DOORS

Desirable HOOSIER features

THE HOOSIER introduced the first kitchen convenience to make it easy to find flavoring extracts, knives, spoons, change, milk tickets and other small articles, by placing special trays for them on the doors.

One of these trays not only makes it easy for the housewife to put her hand on the exact flavoring extract she wants, but keeps the narrow extract bottles from falling over.

HOOSIER doors are also equipped with a handy cookbook holder, which holds the book open on a level with the eyes.

Besides providing these handy trays, the upper doors of the Hoosier Beauty are also equipped with Mrs. Christine Frederick's Patented Food Guide and Salad Chart, grocery want dial, food timer and bill files. These Food Guides and Salad Charts are EXCLUSIVE HOOSIER IMPROVEMENTS.

1927

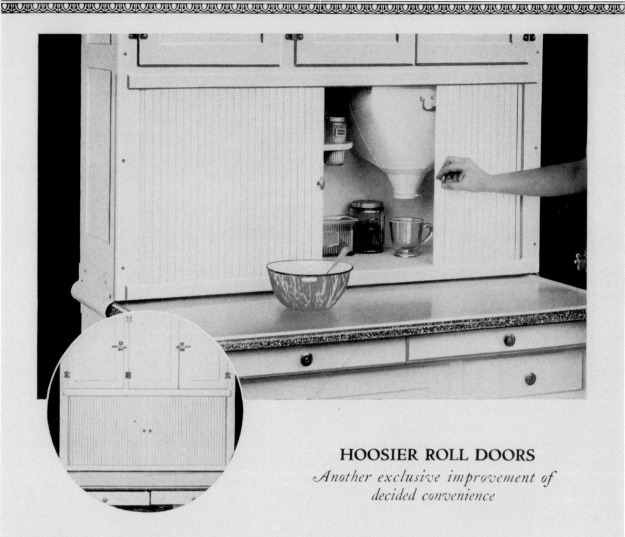

HOOSIER ROLL DOORS

*Another exclusive improvement of
decided convenience*

THE entire door comes out in an instant for cleaning. There are no hidden, inaccessible corners to gather dust and dirt. And there is nothing to stick, bind or get out of order.

When closed, these doors give the HOOSIER a neat, clean appearance. When open, they not only make the flour sifter, spice jars and sugar bins accessible, but expose a big unobstructed cupboard space that adds materially to the working space.

By a special slot in the grooved channel in which the doors slide, these channels are self-cleaning. Crumbs and dust cannot accumulate in them.

The HOOSIER may be had with these removable roll doors, or equipped throughout with hinge doors. See illustration on page 26.

1927

March 16, 1918

September 15, 1917

The interior is just as sanitary. The inside corners are round. No sharp angles where dirt can crowd into and stubbornly stick. But a *round* corner that keeps out disagreeable accumulations and helps keep itself clean.

There are thirty-six other remarkable improvements—new exclusive ideas in Sugar Bins—Flour Bins—Cake Closets, etc. **Greater** and more advantages than can be had in any other make. The best value ever offered.

See this remarkable cabinet at your furniture dealer's today. Be sure to send for Free beautifully illustrated descriptive literature that tells how to save kitchen time, work and money. Most dealers sell "Kitchen Maids" on easy payments.

WASMUTH-ENDICOTT CO., Andrews, Ind.

Warehouses: Kansas City, Mo.;   Omaha, Neb.;   Oakland, Cal.;   Los Angeles, Cal.

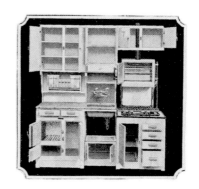

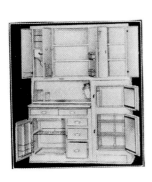

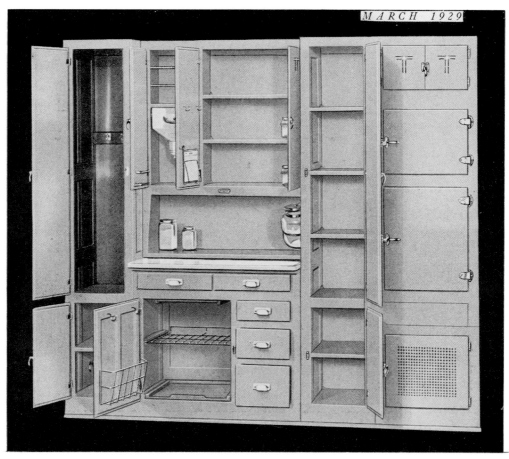

McDougall

A page from the McDougall Cabinet Book "McDougall Kitchen Cabinets", copyright 1906
This cabinet is also pictured on pages 88 & 89 - this is an open view.

Oak

See pages 40-41

No. 2064

This cabinet embodies all of the features essential to a model kitchen cabinet

McDougall

A page from the McDougall Cabinet Book "McDougall Kitchen Cabinets", copyright 1906

Satin Walnut
See pages 14-15

No. 1621

Page 16

McDougall

A page from the McDougall Cabinet Book "McDougall Kitchen Cabinets", copyright 1906

Page 17

No. 1622

Satin Walnut
See pages 14-15

McDougall

Satin Walnut

See pages 14-15

No. 1623

Page 18

A page from the McDougall Cabinet Book "McDougall Kitchen Cabinets", copyright 1906

Page 19

No. 1624

Satin Walnut
See pages 14-15

A page from the McDougall Cabinet Book "McDougall Kitchen Cabinets", copyright 1906

Satin Walnut
See pages 14-15

No. 1625

Page 20

A page from the McDougall Cabinet Book "McDougall Kitchen Cabinets", copyright 1906

Page 21

No. 1626

Satin Walnut
See pages 14-15

A page from the McDougall Cabinet Book "McDougall Kitchen Cabinets", copyright 1906

Satin Walnut
See pages 14-15

No. 1627

Page 22

A page from the McDougall Cabinet Book "McDougall Kitchen Cabinets", copyright 1906

Page 23

No. 1628

Satin Walnut

See pages 14-15

A page from the McDougall Cabinet Book "McDougall Kitchen Cabinets", copyright 1906

Satin Walnut
See pages 24-25

No. 1831

Page 26

A page from the McDougall Cabinet Book "McDougall Kitchen Cabinets", copyright 1906

Page 27

No. 1832

Satin Walnut
See pages 24 25

McDougall

A page from the McDougall Cabinet Book "McDougall Kitchen Cabinets", copyright 1906

Satin Walnut
See pages 24-25

No. 1833

Page 28

A page from the McDougall Cabinet Book "McDougall Kitchen Cabinets", copyright 1906

Page 29   No. 1834   Satin Walnut
See pages 24-25

A page from the McDougall Cabinet Book "McDougall Kitchen Cabinets", copyright 1906

Satin Walnut
See pages 24-25

No. 1835 closed

Page 30

A page from the McDougall Cabinet Book "McDougall Kitchen Cabinets", copyright 1906

Page 31   No. 1835 open   Satin Walnut
See pages 24-25

A page from the McDougall Cabinet Book "McDougall Kitchen Cabinets", copyright 1906

Satin Walnut

No. 1836 closed

See pages 24-25

Page 32

McDougall

A page from the McDougall Cabinet Book "McDougall Kitchen Cabinets", copyright 1906

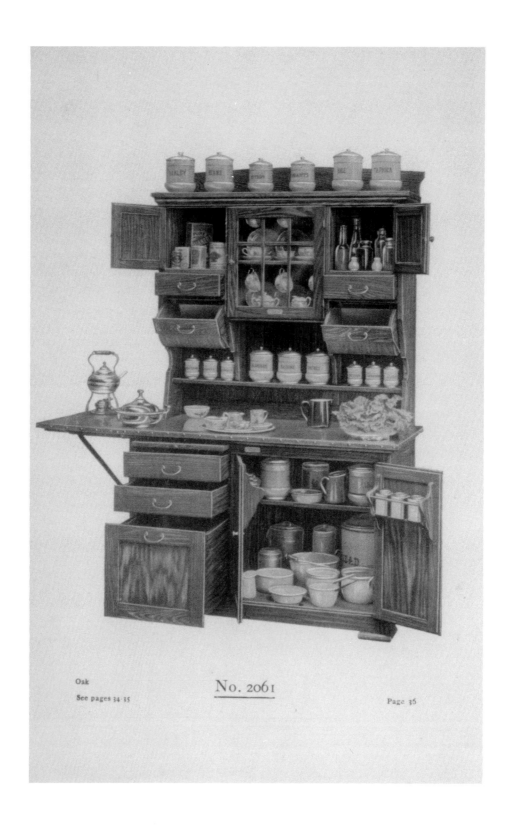

Oak

See pages 34-35

No. 2061

Page 35

A page from the McDougall Cabinet Book "McDougall Kitchen Cabinets", copyright 1906

No. 2063

Oak

Page 37

See pages 34-35

A page from the McDougall Cabinet Book "McDougall Kitchen Cabinets", copyright 1906

Oak

See pages 34-35

No. 2062 closed

Page 38

McDougall

A page from the McDougall Cabinet Book "McDougall Kitchen Cabinets", copyright 1906

No. 2062 open

Page 39

Oak
See pages 34-35

A page from the McDougall Cabinet Book "McDougall Kitchen Cabinets", copyright 1906
This cabinet is also pictured on pages 68 & 89 - this is a closed view.

Oak
See pages 14-15

No. 2064 closed

Page 40

McDougall

A page from the McDougall Cabinet Book "McDougall Kitchen Cabinets", copyright 1906
This cabinet is also pictured on pages 68 & 88 - this is an open view.

No. 2064 open

Oak
See pages 44-35

Page 41

A page from the McDougall Cabinet Book "McDougall Kitchen Cabinets", copyright 1906

Page 43

No. 3071

Oak
See pages 14-35

A page from the McDougall Cabinet Book "McDougall Kitchen Cabinets", copyright 1906

Oak

See pages 44-45

No. 3072

Page 44

A page from the McDougall Cabinet Book "McDougall Kitchen Cabinets", copyright 1906

Page 45   No. 3073   Oak
See pages 34-35

"Of course you'll stay to dinner, Aunt Emily. I've everything from soup to dessert here in my McDougall—and it won't take five minutes to serve."

November, 1919

McDougall originated the idea and made the first Kitchen Cabinet many years ago. McDougall has always created the design and leads in improvements. That is why the McDougall Auto-Front is the undisputed "Steinway of the Kitchen".

Back of the scene of the most successful dinners, luncheons and breakfasts, you will find the McDougall Kitchen Cabinet—helping in a hundred ways to prepare and serve the perfect meal—efficiently—economically. Before you build, write McDougall Company for free plans of Model Modern Kitchens.

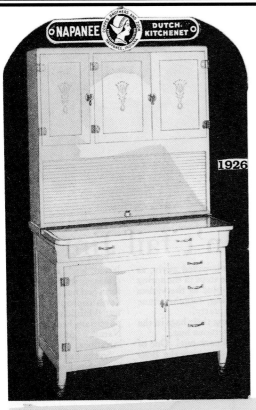

1926

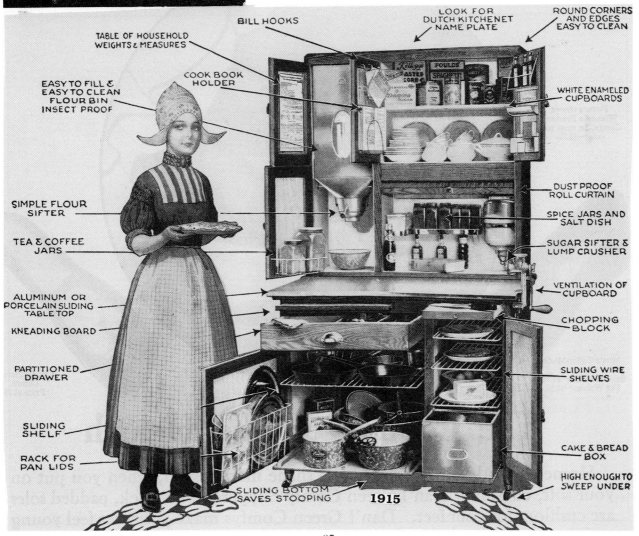

LOOK FOR
DUTCH KITCHENET
NAME PLATE

ROUND CORNERS
AND EDGES
EASY TO CLEAN

BILL HOOKS

TABLE OF HOUSEHOLD
WEIGHTS & MEASURES

COOK BOOK
HOLDER

EASY TO FILL &
EASY TO CLEAN
FLOUR BIN
INSECT PROOF

WHITE ENAMELED
CUPBOARDS

SIMPLE FLOUR
SIFTER

DUST PROOF
ROLL CURTAIN

SPICE JARS AND
SALT DISH

TEA & COFFEE
JARS

SUGAR SIFTER &
LUMP CRUSHER

ALUMINUM OR
PORCELAIN SLIDING
TABLE TOP

VENTILATION OF
CUPBOARD

KNEADING BOARD

CHOPPING
BLOCK

PARTITIONED
DRAWER

SLIDING WIRE
SHELVES

SLIDING
SHELF

RACK FOR
PAN LIDS

CAKE & BREAD
BOX

SLIDING BOTTOM
SAVES STOOPING

HIGH ENOUGH TO
SWEEP UNDER

1915

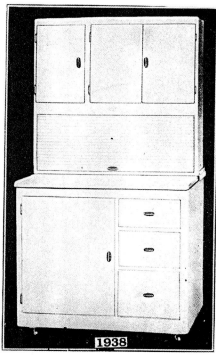

This Napanee beauty, streamlined for today's kitchens, is ideal for use when space is limited. Comes with full set of glassware, bread drawer with cover, dovetailed utility drawers, door basket and kneading board in pan compartment, sliding stainless porcelain top 20x24 inches. Width 24 inches; height 70 inches; weight, 109 lbs.

Here is a full sized cabinet by Napanee with a generous amount of storage space so conveniently arranged that none is wasted. It is completely equipped with a sliding stainless porcelain top, 25x36 inches, large capacity flour bin with sifter, complete set of glassware, dovetailed utility drawers, metal bread drawer with cover, door basket, kneading board and sliding shelf in pan compartment. Width 36 inches; height 70 inches; weight 194 lbs.

Napanee Kitchen Base with 24x20 inch white stainless porcelain top. Has kneading board, large drawer, door basket and shelf in pan compartment. Chromium plated hardware. Comes in choice of white, ivory, or green enamel finishes. Please specify finish desired. Weight 57 lbs.

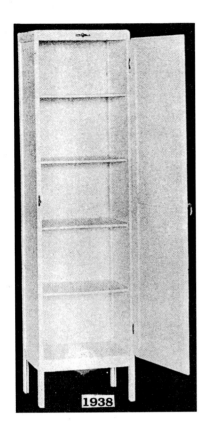

Napanee Utility Closet for kitchen, linen or dishes. Useful in bathroom, hospital or doctors' offices. Finished in choice of White, Green, Ivory or Green and Ivory. Please specify finish desired. Height, 67 inches; width, 18 inches; depth, 13 inches. Weight, 42 lbs. Specify finish desired.

Napanee Kitchen Cabinet, shown to right. Equipped with wood shelf and drawer in upper compartment, a six-piece set of glassware including sugar bowl as shown. Has two metal drawers with covers for flour and for bread; two wood utility drawers. Glassware available in black, red, or crystal. Please specify color desired. Stainless porcelain sliding top. Width 36 inches, height 64 inches. Shipping weight 169 lbs. Please specify finishes.

Here is a very completely equipped cabinet that is designed to fit into modern or old kitchens. It has a 25x40 inch, pull-out stainless porcelain table top, two metal drawers with sliding cover for flour and for bread; two wood utility drawers; six pieces of glassware in crystal color; a very ample pan compartment; and wire door baskets on the inside of all doors. Pulls are black, blue, ivory, green or red. Please specify color of enamel or oak finish as desired. Width 40 inches, height 70 inches. Shipping weight, 200 lbs.

Napanee Broom Cabinet. May be had in the following enamel finishes: White, Green and Ivory, Green or Ivory enamel. Please specify finish desired. Has one top shelf. Height, 67 inches; width, 18 inches; depth, 13 inches. Weight, 37 lbs. Specify finish desired.

A complete cabinet by Napanee that is both compact and modernly styled. Equipped with flour bin, sliding porcelain top 20x30 inches, glassware, metal bread drawer with cover and two dovetailed utility drawers. Large pan compartment with kneading board and wire baskets on doors. Width 30 inches; height 70 inches; weight, 159 lbs.

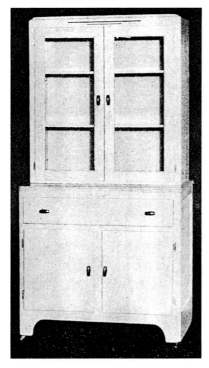

Napanee China Cabinet. Available in either enamel or oak finish described below. Please specify finish desired. Width, 34½ inches; height, 70 inches; depth of base, 18 inches. Shipping weight, 140 lbs.

Napanee Kitchen Base with 22x27 inch white stainless porcelain top. Has two linen drawers, bread drawer and kneading board, chromium plated hardware. A neat compact unit with plenty of storage space. Comes in choice of white, ivory, or green enamel finishes. Please specify finish desired. Weight, 68 lbs.

Sellers Introduction

The G.I. Sellers and Sons Company began manufacturing oak furniture in Kokomo, Indiana in 1888 under the supervision of founder George Ira Sellers. Shortly thereafter, the company took residence in Elwood, Indiana on March 15, 1905, due to a fire which crippled the facility in Kokomo. The city of Elwood offered the defunct facility of the Elwood Planing Mill, a mere twenty miles (as the crow flies) from the original location. George and his son Wilfred purchased the plant, allowing production to resume almost immediately rather than rebuilding the Kokomo plant.

The earliest cabinets produced in the 1800's often had the "dry-sink" style of work top, with the recessed surface board. Soon thereafter, the even "table top" styles proved to be more convenient, as they were designed so the top could be pulled from the upper section of cabinets, increasing the work area. These tops usually were covered with a sheet of nickel metal, yet there also remained work tops made of an inch and a half of maple wood. Later, around 1913, heavy gauge metal prevailed over nickel as the work top surface, coated with electrically fused porcelain. This surface bore the trade name "porceliron". This proved to be quite popular, as it was stainproof and easy to clean.

Sellers cabinets were at first referred to as *Kitcheneed*, then *Mastercraft* and *Klearfront*.

Previous to the metal topped cabinets of 1913 and beyond, all cabinets were coated with an oak colored wood filler, which was immediately rubbed with seaweed until dry. Once the coating was dry, a coat of shellac was applied to the top and base sections in spray booths. After the shellac, the sections were then forwarded to the varnish spray booth. The next part of the process included hand rubbing of the varnished surfaces with cloth-covered blocks dipped in pumice and linseed oil. This was intended to provide protection from steam and moisture.

In addition to the golden oak styled finish, a white enamel line of cabinets was also offered about 1913. This series met instantly with success. Soon, a light gray enamel and a jade green enamel finish was made available. All enamel finishes had several base coats, followed by a finishing coat. The enamel was then baked on in "oven rooms".

"This is the Age of Color" was the theme for the magazine ads and catalogs for Sellers cabinets in 1925. Elegantly designed stenciled decor was painted on the door panels, and new colors of enamel finishes were being offered. In addition to the older finishes of white, jade green, and gray, there were now colors available such as Colonial Ivory and Spanish Tan, plus unnamed oak varnish finishes such as green tinted and amber. A beautiful dark gray (almost black) varnish finish called Silver Gray Oak appeared during this time as well, with flecks of oak grain creating attractive light-colored streaks.

The top sections of Sellers cabinets contained flour bins and a well-made sifter, with a strong bracket for lowering and refilling the flour bin- complete with springs to balance it when being lowered or raised back into place. Racks of several spice jars for a variety of flavors were also enclosed. Behind a vertically raising wooden curtain hid these spice jar racks alongside a large lidded sugar bowl and scoop. On the end of the cabinet base, a bracket was mounted upon which to secure a food chopper.

There were narrow cabinets available for smaller apartment kitchens, with two door upper sections. Larger kitchens could be fitted with three and four foot wide cabinets, bearing three or four door upper sections.

The bases of cabinets were designed with two shallow drawers for towels and luncheon cloths. The right side of the base section had two drawers about six inches deep for tableware and utensils. Below these drawers was a deeper drawer with a metal frame to hold bread and baked goods. This deep drawer had a sliding metal lid and a sliding shelf inside, which was quite handy for dessert items. The base contained a large storage area for pans, kettles, and all the other cooking ware. In this area was a large pullout wire shelf. At the bottom of the storage area was a big flat shelf which connected to the inside of the base door. Handily enough, this shelf automatically extended from the cabinet when the door was opened, enabling the pots and cooking ware to be within arms reach of the cook.

Wildred Sellers designed ant-proof casters for the Sellers cabinets. This consisted of a shallow bowl-shaped disc around the caster which, when filled with water, a light oil, or baking soda, would prevent the access of ants into the cabinet.

In addition to the mobile cabinets which could be maneuvered about the kitchen, Sellers began making a built-in line of kitchen cabinets around 1930. A wide choice of unit sections and sizes was offered, which would be selected by the buyer for a vast range of permanent installations. The Sellers company sold complete kitchen installations for many multi-story apartment hotels throughout the nation, including single, double, or triple basin sink units and also mechanical refrigerators. Full choices of enamel or varnish finishes were available for the built-in line of Sellers cabinets.

Several styles of kitchen work tables were made by the Sellers Company. Cabinet bases without the top sections were available for increased work space. These usually contained base-section drawers. Also there were many styles of drop-leaf and extension-leaf breakfast tables, with chairs for them available in Windsor and other styles.

In addition to the kitchen cabinets, side units of the same height were manufactured. These were about eighteen inches square and had a full length door with a choice of right or left hinges. These had no shelves so as to store brooms and mops more efficiently. Shelves could be added upon request, however, for convenient placing of grocery items and such. These side units had the full choice of varnish and enamel finishes, so as to match the cabinets without mistake.

Oak was the wood used for the varnished cabinets. The enamel cabinets were made of gum wood, magnolia, and poplar. Truckloads of lumber were stacked outside for seasoning, in piles about six or eight feet high. One inch slats were positioned between each layer of lumber, allowing air to circulate among the stack. After days of seasoning, the lumber was maneuvered upon transfer platforms, along a series of tracks which led into large rooms containing drying kilns. A controlled system of steam pipes removed moisture from the lumber before it was introduced to the woodworking machines. This was to prevent any warping or swelling of the wood during or after sawing, planing, or sanding.

After the assembly and the enamel or varnish finishes had been completed, employees at work stations would apply drawer knobs, door hinges, mounted shelves, and all the other finishing parts. Cooking charts and a card was affixed inside the doors of the top section. One card had black metal pointers for reminders of grocery items, plus a small "hourglass" egg timer filled with red sand.

Month after month, four color ads appeared in such magazines as *Ladies Home Journal*, *Good Housekeeping*, *Saturday Evening Post*, and *American Builder*. There was a plentiful supply of advertising illustrations available for dealers to provide for newspaper advertisements. A wide range of advertising window display material, sale bills, and envelope stuffers was made available to local salespeople as well, with catalogs being sent directly from the factory to those responding to magazine advertisements.

The Sellers company had 4500 retail store dealers throughout the country, and 48 travelling salesmen continually called upon the dealers offering services and new products.

A permanent display suite was located at the Merchandise Mart in Chicago, and Sellers participated every year at the Furniture Show at High Point, North Carolina.

A nice brick structure was built on 13th street in Elwood, located across from the factory itself, which displayed many of the furnishings supplied by the Sellers company. Four separate kitchens (complete with household sinks) with different arrangements provided display sites for several various models of cabinets and breakfast sets for dealers to examine.

Each year all the travelling salesmen came to Elwood for a two week sales "school". At these "schools", the company would demonstrate and show off all the new styles and features available.

Railway switches were at the factory for direct loading of full railcar capacity. Several sales campaigns sent out trains pulling over 100 cars loaded with Sellers kitchen furniture only.

Sellers cabinets were designed to be- and were advertised as- "The Best Servant In Your House".

Dull Golden Oak Finish

The Sellers
35B

This Sellers model has many features for a small family home. It is made with a golden oak finish. It comes in either porceliron or aluminum work table on rollers, with a horizontal roll curtain front, ant-proof casters, and glass drawer pulls.

The 35B measures 70 inches high on the casters. It is 42 inches wide and gives you a working space of 38 X 41 inches when the work table is fully extended. This cabinet has ample storage space and is delightfully convenient for the smaller family.

November. 1919

Sellers "Special"

Has the patented automatic lowering flour bin and other features listed. Dimensions are 70 x 42 inches on ant-proof casters. It has 38 x 41 inch working surface when table is fully extended. Most complete kitchen cabinet ever designed.

Sellers Special
Width 42 inches—Height
70 inches. Leader of all
standard sized cabinets.
White enamel or golden oak.

1921

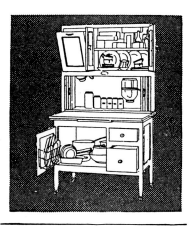

Sellers No. 435
Width 42 inches—Height
70 inches. A serviceable
low-priced cabinet. Oak.

Sellers Majestic
Width 48 inches—Height
81 inches. The biggest and
roomiest Sellers made—
white enameled.

Sellers No. 50
Width 42 inches—Height
70 inches. A high-grade
popular-priced cabinet.
White enamel or golden oak.

Shown on this page
are a descriptive list of
some of the cabinet mod-
els used in 1921.

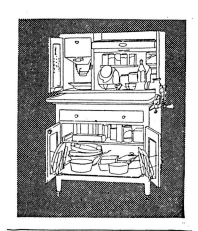

Sellers Apartment No. 32
Width 36 inches—Height
54 inches. Beautiful white
enamel—fits small space.

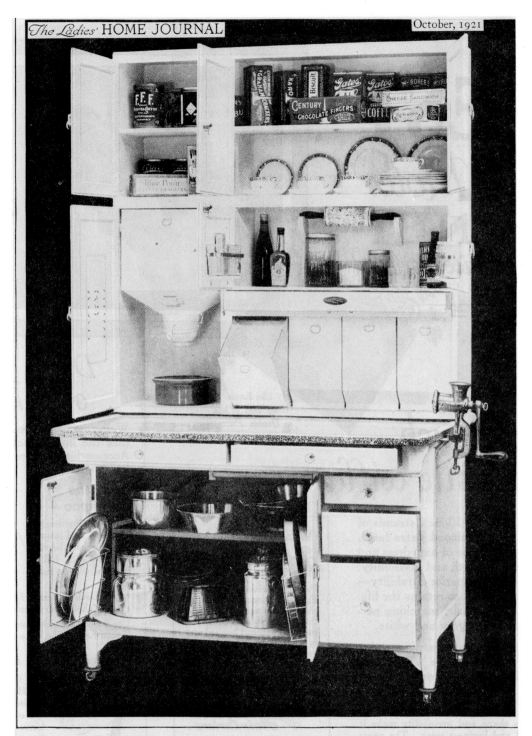

ANNOUNCING
The New SELLERS *Majestic*

The "Majestic" was Sellers largest cabinet made, it stood 81 inches high and had a width of 48". Shown above is the white enameled model.

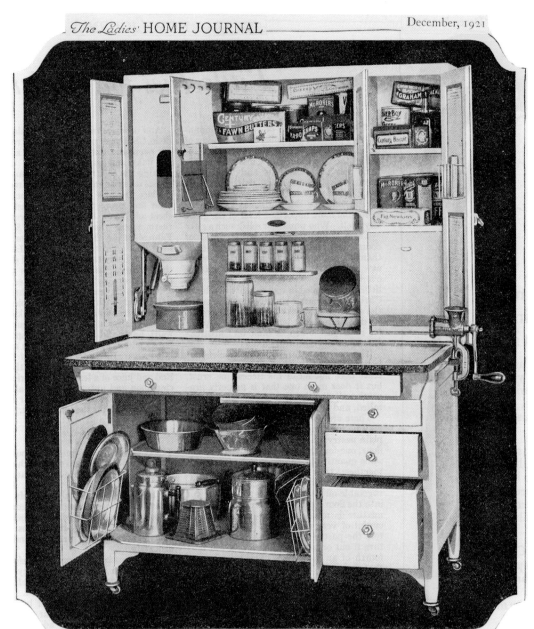

The Ladies' HOME JOURNAL ———————— December, 1921

Sellers Mastercraft
Width 48 inches —Height 70 inches. A fine cabinet of large capacity. White enamel or golden oak.

   This "Mastercraft" with the two cutlery drawers, with features that include: Glass Knobs, Ant-Proof Casters, Porceliron
Table and Pull Down Design Flour Bin.

The "Mastercraft" cabinet above shows the patented lowering flour bin.

Shown here are the glass knobs, ant-proof casters and dove tail joints used in the fastening of wood in "Sellers" cabinets.

Shown is the porceliron top.

Bottom slide out drawer.

This Sellers "Mastercraft" was made in white enamel. The features included are: glass knobs, porceliron top, ant-proof casters, pull-out flour and sugar bins and a bottom shelf extender.

Width – 48"

Height – 70"

Note: Some differences in other "Mastercraft" cabinets are the cutlery drawers under the work computer, some have one drawer as shown here, while others have two.

Sellers

$59⁵⁰

f. o. b.
Elwood, Ind.

This popular model, No. 30-45, is 42 inches wide, 71 inches high and 25 inches deep. Has a removable 30-pound metal flour bin, automatic base shelf extender, extending porceliron worktable, ant-proof casters, glass drawer pulls, wedged tenon dovetail construction, three-point non-jamming drawers, metal bread box drawer and 8-piece glassware set. Finished in steam- and climate-proof Sellers Gray Satin-White, Jade Green or Ivory Enamels, all handsomely decorated. Also in Amber Oak and Silver-Gray Oak.

... Note to the right the units that make up the beautiful installation illustrated below. No. 1 is a broom closet. No. 2 is a utility closet with shelves. No. 3 is the upper master section with flour bin, storage shelves and "KLEARFront." No. 4 is the master base with porceliron work table. No. 5 is a storage cabinet. No. 6 is a refrigerator—for natural ice or mechanical refrigeration. This is only one of almost unlimited combinations possible for kitchens of every size.

September 21, 1929

September 21, 1929

These two Seller's units were advertising the individual units being sold to the public to suit their lifestyles.

April 1928 Good Housekeeping

When building or remodeling —consider Sellers Sectional Built-in Units for your kitchen. Now being used in many expensive homes and exclusive apartment buildings. Write for information.

The colorful kitchen is *more* than *stylish* ·· it is *inspiring!*

SURROUNDINGS have everything to do with our dispositions. Consider the woman who works in a bleak, cheerless kitchen. How can she be bright and cheery? How can her kitchen duties be inspiring? What she needs is a bright, colorful, garden spot of a room.

That is why the new, stylish, colorful Sellers kitchen has so quickly become popular. It met a crying need in thousands of homes. It has literally transfigured countless weary women by bringing sunshine and joy into hours that were often sour and irksome.

Sellers, through the new, colorful, stylish Kitchenaires, offers a very simple way to make any kitchen beautiful.

With a Sellers Kitchenaire in rich Jade Green, dainty Colonial Ivory, Sellers Grey, Spanish Gold, one may have a colorful kitchen at small expense.

In many beautiful homes, most elaborate colorful kitchens are planned to include a fashionable

Sellers Kitchen Ensemble—cabinet, utility closets and breakfast set all done in the same exquisite colors and decorative motif.

And do not forget that the Sellers, while dressed in new and stylish colors, is primarily the greatest of all time- and labor-savers in the kitchen.

In it you will find all of those many ingenious improvements and devices that have made "Sellers" famous in millions of homes.

Bring the joy of color and beauty into your kitchen hours. As a first step go see these new stylish, colorful Sellers Kitchenaires at the local dealer's store. The prices are very moderate. Most dealers sell on very *easy terms.*

We have a catalog for you

Our new catalog, just off the press, is a beautiful book. Shows many attractive colorful kitchen ideas. Also shows the Sellers Kitchenaire in realistic colors. We have a copy ready for you, but we do not have your address. Will you send it?

G. I. SELLERS & SONS CO.
Dept. 204, Elwood, Indiana

SELLERS GREY

COLONIAL IVORY

SPANISH GOLD

SERVER IN JADE GREEN

SELLERS
KITCHENAIRE

No. 30-87 can be had in these finishes beautifully decorated:

Two-tone Green Oak
Shaded Amber Oak
Silver Oak
Light Amber Oak
    (not shaded)
Jade Green Enamel
Satin White Enamel
Colonial Ivory
    Enamel (illus.)
Sellers Gray Enamel

Sellers KlearFront No. 30-87 shown with the doors opened and curtain up. The 12-piece glassware set illustrated is regular equipment with this model.

Sellers *Klear*Front No. 30-87

In this beautifully proportioned cabinet you offer your customers the utmost in beauty, utility and convenience. No other cabinet contains so many labor- and time-saving conveniences. Yet this cabinet sells at a price within everybody's means. This cabinet contains all of the 15 famous features (see pages 14 and 15).

Your customers will like its big expanse of snow-white porceliron working surface, free from swinging doors, gutters and other obstructions—the porceliron covered bottom shelf in upper section that protects forever the part which in ordinary cabinets first becomes unsightly. This feature adds nearly fifty per cent more porceliron working surface. They will like its superb fine furniture finish. Its cutlery drawers which extend with the porceliron table top. And its base shelf which extends automatically when the base door is opened. No. 30-87 is 42 inches wide, 71 inches high and 25 inches deep.

1930 Catalog Page

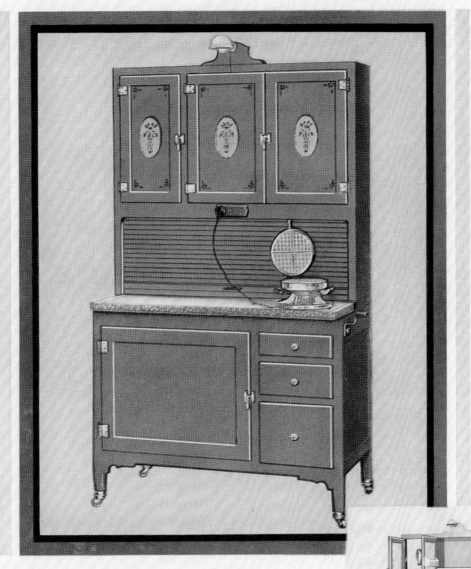

No. 30-65 can be had in these finishes beautifully decorated:

Two-tone Green Oak

Shaded Amber Oak

Silver Oak

Light Amber Oak (not shaded)

Jade Green Enamel (illus.)

Satin White Enamel

Colonial Ivory Enamel

Sellers Gray Enamel

Sellers Electric *Klear*Front No. 30-65

Electricity is used for many things in the modern home today. Many housewives are seriously inconvenienced by not having a sufficient number of electrical outlets to hook up all of their appliances. This electric model is wired and designed to overcome this difficulty. The Utili-tap in the front of the cabinet supplies outlets for three appliances at one time.

This cabinet also is equipped with electric shade and fixture at the top of the cabinet. This lighting fixture can be had on any other Sellers Cabinet at a slight additional cost.

In this Sellers Electric Cabinet you will find the many features for which Sellers is famous. Including full width *Klear*Front, curtain that rolls up and disappears, automatic base shelf extender, drawers that cannot stick or jam even in wet weather, etc. No. 30-65 is 42 inches wide, 71 inches high and 25 inches deep.

Electric KlearFront No. 30-65 with doors open and curtain up. The 8-piece glassware set illustrated is regular equipment with this cabinet.

No. 30-45 can be had in these finishes beautifully decorated:

Silver Oak
(illustrated)
Shaded Amber Oak
Two-tone Green Oak
Light Amber Oak
(not shaded)
Jade-Green Enamel
Sellers Gray Enamel
Satin-White Enamel
Colonial Ivory
Enamel

Sellers *KlearFront* No. 30-45

Isn't this Silver Oak a beautiful finish? Notice the two-toned effect —colorful and yet soft and effeminate. Showing through its glorious finish is the unmistakable Oak grain. What a potent word Oak is in selling furniture! It stands for strength—long-wearing qualities.

In these new finishes Sellers give you the selling power of Oak combined with new alluring beauty. These charming new Oak finishes are in keeping with the new trend toward softer colors and tints. You are buying them on a rising market—a market which will grow rapidly under the impetus of Sellers national advertising. The cabinet illustrated is the most popular model in the Sellers line—a cabinet of unusual quality at a sensational price.

No. 30-45 with the doors open and curtains un. Observe its ample storage space and work table free from swinging doors.

1930 Catalog Page

No. 30-23 can be had in these finishes beautifully decorated:

Two-tone Green Oak

Shaded Amber Oak (illustrated)

Silver Oak

Light Amber Oak (not shaded)

Satin-White Enamel

Jade-Green Enamel

Sellers Gray Enamel

*The interior of the upper section of No. 30-23 is the same as No. 30-45, except that it is 6 inches less in width. The base has a wire shelf, and also a wire pan rack on base door.

Utility Closets can be had in all colors to match Sellers Cabinets.

No. 39 S   No. 39 BC

Sellers Utility Closets with doors open showing the abundant storage space they afford.

Sellers *KlearFront No. 30-23**

This genuine Sellers Cabinet establishes a new low-priced value for quality merchandise. It is built entirely of hardwood and can be had in a wide range of beautiful colors. Dimensions—36 inches wide, 71 inches high, 25 inches deep.

The two Utility Closets shown with this cabinet can be had in any color to match with Sellers Kitchen Cabinets. Because of the many uses they can be put to, you have a tremendous market for these Closets. Nearly every kitchen needs one or more of them. No. 39 S is furnished with full size shelves. No. 39 BC is equipped with shelves and with space for brooms, vacuum cleaner, etc. Dimensions on both models— 71 inches high, 19 inches wide, 12⅜ inches deep.

Sellers Kitchen Tables

in four charming colors

Beautiful New Sellers Breakfast Buffet —No. 3004

Finished in—

Shaded Amber Oak	Jade Green Enamel
Two-tone Green Oak	Colonial Ivory Enamel
Silver Oak	Sellers Gray Enamel

Now you can have Kitchen Tables in four joyful colors. All Sellers Tables can be had in these colors—Jade Green Enamel and Colonial Ivory Enamel with decorative brown edge porceliron tops —Sellers Gray Enamel and Satin-White Enamel with decorative green edge porceliron tops. Combined with this beauty of color is the sturdiness of Sellers construction. Fruit acids will not injure the sanitary porceliron tops on Sellers Tables, for they are finished exactly like the work table of Sellers Kitchen Cabinets.

The drawer in each table is divided into two convenient compartments. The drawer is equipped with a sparkling crystal glass drawer pull that will never tarnish. The gracefully tapered legs which add so much to the beauty of the table, are

The New Sellers Buffet

Sellers has designed a Buffet of unusual charm and beauty to complete the Sellers Breakfast Suites. It is Sellers' exclusive wedge tenon dovetail construction throughout, assuring strength and durability found in no other buffet. The gracefully turned legs match those of all Sellers Breakfast Suites. Drop pulls of distinctive design on doors and drawers. Two 14 inch drawers and two 12 inch doors. Finished and decorated in all colors to match Sellers Breakfast Suites. 44 inches wide, 15 inches deep, 35½ inches high.

attached with nuts, easily kept tight. All finishes are steam and climate proof. Comes in three sizes:

No. 305—24 x 36 inches
No. 306—25 x 40½ inches
No. 308—25 x 48 inches

1930 Catalog Page

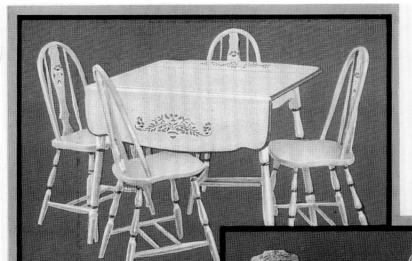

No. 309 Table—No. 32 Chair
To left

No. 303 Table—No. 34 Chair
Below

Sellers Drop-Leaf Breakfast Suites

Sellers Drop-Leaf Breakfast Suite No. 309—Chair No. 32 illustrated

A charming drop-leaf suite that is fine furniture in design and finish. The table extended measures 38 by 42 inches and is a compact 38 by 21 inches when the leaves are dropped. Has a 5-ply top with knuckle-jointed leaves supported by four strong hinges. Any of the chairs illustrated can be had with this suite. All chairs have Sellers glue-key joint construction that cannot come apart and are machine leveled. Finishes: Jade Green, Gray or Ivory Enamels and Shaded Amber Oak, Silver Oak, Two-tone Green Oak and Jade Green Enamel base with Walnut top.

Sellers Drop-Leaf Breakfast Suite No. 303 Chair No. 34 illustrated above

Compare this Breakfast Set with any other set and you will immediately see what an ex-

Open Cupboard No. 3001
Sellers Open Cupboard can be had in all finishes to match Sellers Breakfast Sets. 66½ inches high. 38 inches wide and 17 inches deep. The closed Cupboard is shown on page 11.

traordinary value it is. In this set you find the superb Sellers finish — Sellers construction—Sellers high quality materials — all combined in a breakfast set selling at a sensationally low price. This set is hardwood throughout. solid wood top amply braced and reinforced. The leaves are knuckle-jointed. The table is 38 by 42 inches extended. The chairs have glue-key joints that will not pull apart. Legs are machine leveled. Finishes: Jade Green, Sellers Gray and Colonial Ivory Enamels.

1930 Catalog Page

Can be had in these beautifully decorated finishes:

Jade-Green Enamel with walnut top (illustrated)

All Jade Green Enamel

Colonial Ivory Enamel

Sellers Gray Enamel

Shaded Amber Oak

Two-tone Green Oak

Silver Oak

Sellers Extension Dinette
Table No. 300
Chair No. 33

Closed Cupboard No. 3002

Sellers Cupboards in both open and closed models can be had in all finishes to match Breakfast Sets. 66½ inches high, 38 inches wide, 17 inches deep.

Open Cupboard shown on page 12.

Here is a Dinette that will appeal to newly married couples who are just starting to keep house or to those with small dining rooms.

The table top pulls apart at the center and a hinged leaf swings up into place when you wish to extend the length of the table. The extension action is extremely easy because of the patented metal slides.

It moves at touch of finger. 32 inches wide and 42½ inches long when closed. Extended it is 32 inches by 60 inches. Can be had with the chairs illustrated or with chairs shown on next page.

The Utili-Tap—3 Way Extension Outlet

Now that so many things are prepared electrically at the table, more electric outlets are needed. All Sellers

Breakfast Sets can be had with this richly finished three-way outlet at a small extra cost. Three appliances can be operated from it at the same time.

1930 Catalog Page

Above—Sellers Base Unit No. 30-87

Sellers Base Units

Some kitchens do not have the wall space required by a kitchen cabinet. For these kitchens Sellers has built Base Units. These useful units will fit under any window or under built-in hanging cupboards. The Base Unit offers all of the conveniences found in the bases of Sellers Kitchen Cabinets. A top shelf is provided on each model for the glassware sets which are regular equipment.

No. 30-87 Base is 37⅜ inches high, 42 inches wide, 25 inches deep. It has cutlery drawers that extend with porceliron top, automatic extending base shelf, 12-piece glassware set and all other features found in the base of Cabinet No. 30-87.

No. 30-45 Base is 37⅜ inches high, 42 inches wide, 25 inches deep. Has extending porceliron top, automatic extending base shelf, 8-piece glassware set, etc.

No. 30-23 Base is 37⅜ inches high, 36 inches wide, 25 inches deep. Has extending porceliron top and 8-piece glassware set.

No. 30-45 Base

No. 30-23 Base

1930 Catalog Page

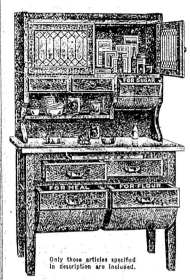

Only those articles specified in description are included.

Only those articles specified in description are included.

Only those articles specified in description are included.

Made of seasoned maple in natural maple or golden finish, as noted in price list below. Entire height, 62 in.
Has a roomy cupboard for dishes, packages, canned goods, supplies, etc., extends the entire width of the cabinet. Frosted glass paneled doors. The two small drawers are convenient for spices, small kitchen sundries, etc. Sugar bin tilts forward.
The top of base is 25x42 inches, made of white basswood, the ideal wood for kitchen cabinet tops. Also, furnished with metal covered top, as quoted below. Two large bins have wood bottoms and each has ample capacity; one is for flour and the other for corn meal. Two drawers above bins, one for linen, the other for cutlery. Removable kneading and chopping board. Steel sliding casters. Shipped knocked down from factory near CHICAGO. Shipping weight, about 145 pounds.

	Natural	Golden
No. 1L2122½	Finish	Finish
Price, with white basswood top	$10.45	$10.48
Price, with metal covered top	12.45	12.48

Made of seasoned oak in the light golden finish. This finish gives the cabinet a bright, clean appearance and is the most popular finish for oak kitchen cabinets. Height, 68 inches.
Top has two roomy china and storage cupboards, each fitted with a shelf and fancy glass paneled door. Two small drawers for small kitchen sundries, four smaller drawers for spices. Sugar bin with a roomy shelf on each side.
Large top, 25x42 inches, made of white basswood, the ideal wood for kitchen cabinet tops. Also furnished with metal covered top as listed below. Roomy cupboard for pots and pans, has a sliding shelf and the door is fitted with a large rack for pot lids, pans, etc. Has two drawers, one useful for cutlery, the other for kitchen linen. The large flour bin pulls forward; ample flour capacity. Brass finish metal drawer pulls. Removable kneading and chopping board. Shipped from factory near CHICAGO. Shipping weight, about 230 pounds.
No. 1L2135½ Price, with white basswood top.$15.95
Price, with metal covered top.. 17.95

Made of seasoned maple in choice of natural maple or golden finish, as noted in price list. Entire height, 64 in.
The generous cupboard and drawer spaces make this an exceptionally practical kitchen cabinet. Roomy cupboard for dishes, packages, canned goods, supplies, etc., extends the entire width of the cabinet. The three small drawers are convenient for spices, small kitchen sundries, etc.
The top of the base is 25x42 inches, made of white basswood, the ideal wood for kitchen cabinet tops. Also furnished with metal covered top as quoted below. The two large bins have wood bottoms and each has ample capacity; one can be used for flour and the other for corn meal, if desired. Two drawers above bins, one for linen, the other for cutlery. Removable kneading and chopping board. Legs fitted with steel sliding casters. Shipped knocked down from factory near CHICAGO. Shipping weight, about 145 pounds.

	Natural Finish	Golden Finish
No. 1L2123½		
Price, with white basswood top	$9.85	$9.88
Price, with metal covered top	11.85	11.88

Save Miles of Steps With This Wilson Kitchen Cabinet

$21 65

WITH METAL COVERED TOP.

A Phenomenal Bargain. Here is an opportunity to buy a fine big improved roll curtain front Kitchen Cabinet at a very low price. You will readily recognize the superior arrangement and equipment of this splendid design, the same type of cabinet that is now being extensively advertised and sold throughout the country at much higher prices.

Superior Construction. Made of selected seasoned oak in the natural light dull golden finish. This finish presents a bright cleanly appearance and is the most popular finish for oak cabinets. Inside of china cupboard and space below it are white enameled with a hard durable washable finish, a very important sanitary feature. Other special features are the sanitary steel wire racks and shelves. This cabinet is 72 inches high, 42 inches wide and 26 inches deep when it is closed. The sliding extension top slides forward, increasing the working surface to 38x42 inches. When closed it passes beneath lower shelf at bottom of top section. The regular equipment is metal covered top. Heavy sheet metal is drawn tightly over the strong wood top and securely fastened beneath the edges. As noted below, we also furnish this cabinet with a steel white porcelain enameled top, as described and illustrated in description of No. 1H2149½ above. The porcelain enameled top makes an ideal equipment, and after you have used it you will be glad you paid the extra first cost. Every drawer, bin, top and work board of this cabinet can be removed for cleaning and airing. The small illustration shows how attractive it is when closed. Fine quality nickel finished metal pulls and patent catches. Big wheel casters. Shipped from factory in INDIANA. Shipping weight, about 165 pounds.

Cabinet Closed.
No. 1H2155½ Price, with metal covered top $21.65
Price, with white porcelain enameled top. 24.65

The Flour Bin. Made of metal with sifter on bottom. Large glass view hole in front. Closed top, swings out and fills from back. Dustproof. Ample flour capacity.

The China Cupboard In top is convenient for kitchen dishes, packages, canned goods, supplies, etc. White enameled. **Steel Wire Racks** A Special Sanitary Feature.

Swinging Sugar Bin Made of crystal glass with metal top and patent dispenser on bottom. Swings out on heavy metal arm. Holds about 5 pounds of sugar.

Roll Curtain Front. Dustproof, easy sliding. Gives easy access to this much used section of cabinet.

Coffee, Tea, Salt and Spice Jars. Made of fluted crystal glass with aluminum light fitting screw caps. Four spice jars.

Sliding Extension Top. Slides forward, enlarging working surface to 38x42 inches.

The Work Board In slot underneath the sliding top has two surfaces.

Two Drawers. The top one is divided into three compartments. The bottom one is for kitchen linen.

Large Cutlery Drawer. Above base cupboard is large drawer divided for cutlery and small utensils.

The Large Cupboard Provides large space for pots, pans and larger kitchen utensils. Steel wire sliding shelf.

The Bread and Cake Box Made of metal with sliding perforated lid. Slides forward on wood frame.

Only articles specified are included with cabinet.

1906

Only Articles Specified Are Included With Cabinet.

The Wilson "Perfection"

$23.85 WITH METAL COVERED TOP

You will readily recognize the superior arrangement and equipment of this splendid design, the same type of cabinet that is now being extensively advertised and sold throughout the country at much higher prices.

A Dozen Special Features.

The Flour Bin—Made of metal with sifter on bottom. Large glass view hole in front. Closed top, swings out and fills from back. Dustproof. Ample flour capacity.

The China Cupboard in top is convenient for kitchen dishes, packages, canned goods, supplies, etc. White enameled.

Steel Wire Racks—A Special Sanitary Feature.

Swinging Sugar Bin made of crystal glass with metal top and patent dispenser on bottom. Swings out on heavy metal arm. Holds about 5 pounds of sugar.

Roll Curtain Front—Dustproof, easy sliding. Gives easy access to this much used section of cabinet.

Coffee, Tea, Salt and Spice Jars—Made of fluted crystal glass with aluminum tight fitting screw caps. Four spice jars.

Sliding Extension Top—Slides forward, enlarging working surface to 38x42 inches.

The Work Board in slot underneath the sliding top has two surfaces.

Two Drawers—The top one is divided into three compartments. The bottom one is for kitchen linen.

Large Cutlery Drawer—Above base cupboard is large drawer divided for cutlery and small utensils.

The Large Cupboard provides large space for pots, pans and larger kitchen utensils. Steel wire sliding shelf. Bottom slides forward like drawer.

The Bread and Cake Box—Made of metal with sliding perforated lid. Slides forward on wood frame.

Made of selected seasoned oak in the natural light dull golden finish. This finish presents a bright cleanly appearance and is the most popular finish for oak cabinets. Inside of china cupboard and space below it are white enameled with a hard durable washable finish, a very important sanitary feature. Other special features are the sanitary steel wire racks and shelves. This cabinet is 70 inches high, 42 inches wide and 26 inches deep when top is closed. The sliding extension top slides forward, increasing the working surface to 38x42 inches. When closed it passes beneath lower shelf at bottom of top section. The regular equipment is metal covered top. Heavy sheet metal is drawn tightly over the strong wood top and securely fastened beneath the edges. As noted below, we also furnish this cabinet with a steel white porcelain enameled top, as described and illustrated in description of No. 1L2148½ below. The porcelain enameled top makes an ideal equipment, and after you have used it you will be glad you paid the extra first cost. Every drawer, bin, top and work board of this cabinet can be removed for cleaning and airing. Fine quality nickel finished metal pulls and patent catches. Big wheel casters. Shipped from factory in INDIANA. Shipping weight, about 265 pounds.

Cabinet Closed.

No. 1L2155½
Price, with metal covered top.....................$23.85
Price, with white porcelain enameled top.........27.85

The Wilson "Leader"

$23.95 WITH PORCELAIN ENAMELED TOP

This is one of the most striking values we have ever offered in this line. This cabinet is built of solid oak and constructed to meet the demand for quality and efficiency at a moderate price. It is built in one of the largest furniture factories in the country, where standardized methods and large production make for quality and price reduction.

Note These Many Special Features.

China Cupboard white enameled inside. Steel wire shelf and fancy paneled doors. For kitchen dishes, packages, etc.

Swinging Sugar Bin made of crystal glass with metal cap and dispenser on bottom. Holds about 5 pounds. Swings on heavy metal arm.

Four Spice Jars in steel wire rack on right hand door. Made of crystal fluted glass. Tight fitting screw caps and spaces for labels.

The Two Drawers—The top one is useful for cutlery and the lower one for linen. They are easy sliding and are finished inside.

Bread and Cake Drawer made of metal with sliding ventilated lid. Provides clean, sanitary storage place for bread, cake and pastry.

The Flour Bin tilts forward when filling. Made of metal with patent sifter and panel front. Ample flour capacity.

The Sliding Top—Easy to clean, durable and sanitary; always smooth and level. Slides forward increasing working surface to 38x42 inches.

Steel Wire Rack underneath china cupboard for small packages and rolling pin.

Coffee, Tea and Salt Jars are in steel wire rack in left hand door. Made of crystal fluted glass and have tight metal caps.

The Work Board is in the top of top drawer; removable; two working surfaces.

Large Base Cupboard provides space for pots, pans, etc. Steel wire shelf which slides forward. Bottom slides forward like drawer.

The Pan Rack on base cupboard door is made of steel wire.

Porcelain Enameled Top.

White Porcelain Enameled Top—If preferred, we can furnish this cabinet with a heavy metal white porcelain enameled top, as shown in small illustration. This top has the same hard, durable surface as fine white porcelain enameled cooking ware and makes the ideal kitchen cabinet top. It is snow white, easy to keep clean and absolutely sanitary and far superior in every way to any other kind of cabinet top. After you have used this cabinet for awhile you will be glad you paid the extra cost to get it.

Cabinet Closed.

This is a Wilson Cabinet, made of selected clear grain seasoned oak in a dull satin finish in the light natural oak color. Height, 70 inches; width, 42 inches; depth, with top closed, 25 inches. Top when extended increases working surface to 38x42 inches. China cupboard and section below it are white enameled. Three-ply built up panels used throughout. Big wheel casters. Every drawer, bin and shelf can be removed for cleaning and airing. Shipped from factory in INDIANA. Shipping weight, about 250 pounds.

No. 1L2148⅓
Price, with metal covered top..............$19.95
Price, with white porcelain enameled top..........23.95

1906

Only Articles Specified Are Included With Cabinet.

The Wilson "Special"

$28 65

WITH PORCELAIN ENAMELED TOP

1906

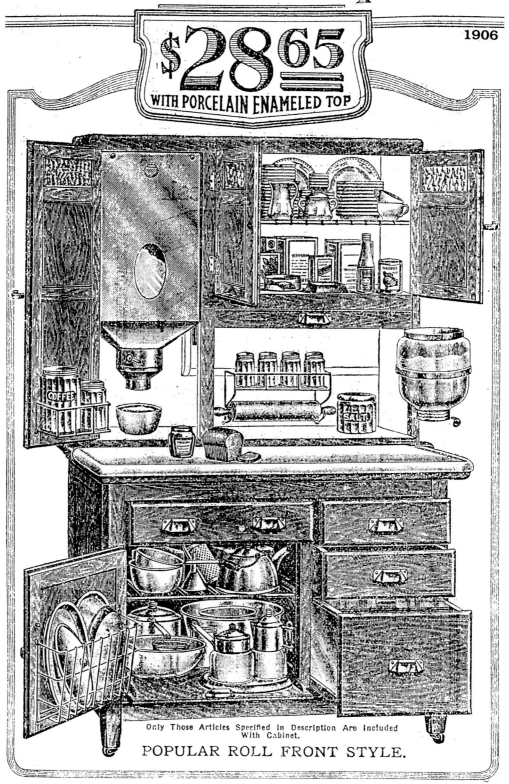

Only Those Articles Specified in Description Are Included
With Cabinet.

POPULAR ROLL FRONT STYLE.

The Wilson "Ideal"

$20⁹⁵ WITH METAL TOP

1906

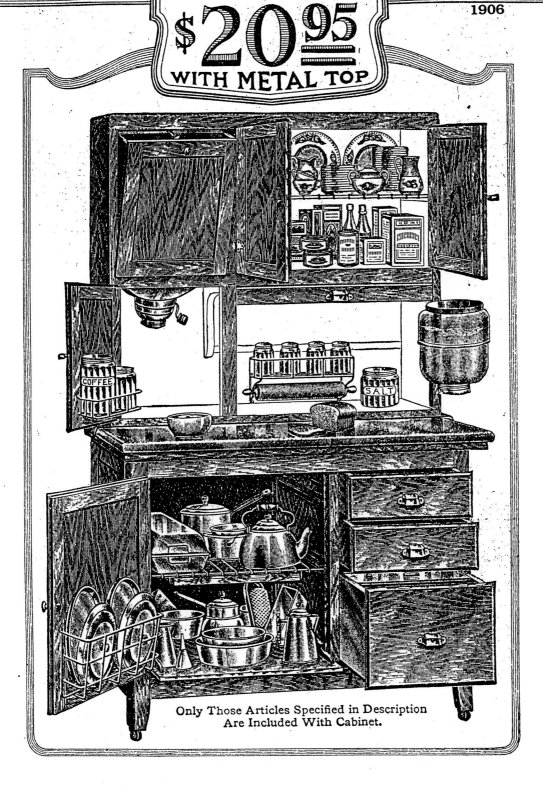

Only Those Articles Specified in Description
Are Included With Cabinet.

The Wilson "Wonder"

$21⁴⁵
WITH BASSWOOD TOP

1906

FOR SUGAR

FOR SALT

COFFEE

FOR FLOUR

FOR MEAL

Only the Spice, Tea and Coffee Cans Are Included
With Cabinet.

This Sellers cabinet has etched glass doors and a 48" wide base, circa 1910s.

This Sellers "Mastercraft" has a 48" wide base, circa 1920s.

Sellers – circa 1920s.

This Sellers "Klearfront" has a
48" wide base, circa 1920s.

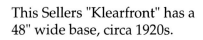

This Sellers has a blue double porcelain top, circa 1920s.

This Sellers was factory painted and is mixed wood, circa 1920s.

Napanee cabinet, circa 1920s.

Napanee cabinet, circa 1920s

McDougall cabinet, circa 1920s.

McDougall cabinet, circa 1920s.

Very unusual oak finished cabinet with numerous small drawers, and a metal work counter. Unfortunately there was not enough information obtained to list manufacturer or other qualities of this cabinet.

McDougall cabinet, circa 1920s.

Hoosier cabinet, circa mid 1920s.

The two pictures to the right are of a Hoosier cabinet. The close-up view is showing the various tins, cookbooks, and the pull-out flour bin. This photo is courtesy of Carol Ellis. She was kind enough to send us a picture of her cabinet.

The two pictures above is of a Hoosier cabinet, showing an open and closed view, circa 1920s.

Price Guide

Page 5: Top - $1250-1500
Middle - $350-500
Bottom - $450-600

Page 6: $1400-1600

Page 10: Top Left - $1800-2200
Top Right - $2500+
Middle - $2500+
Bottom - $2750+

Page 11: Top - $1200-1300
Bottom - $2750+

Page 12: $1300-1500

Page 13: $1400-1700

Page 14: RARE

Page 15: $1300-1500

Page 16: $1300-1500

Page 17: $1000-1200

Page 18: $1300-1500

Page 19: $2600+

Page 20: $1400-1600

Page 21: $1000-1200

Page 22: $1300-1500

Page 23: $2350+
Highboy movable side units - $400-550

Page 24: $2350+

Page 25: 2350+

Page 26: $1000-1200

Page 27: $300-500

Page 28: $300-500

Page 29: Left: $300-450 Right: $250-400

Page 30: $400-600

Page 31: $250-300

Page 32: $250-400

Page 33: $1300-1500

Page 34: $1300-1500

Page 35: $1000-1300

Page 36: $2300+

Page 37: $2000-2300

Page 38: $2400+

Page 39: $1700-1900

Page 40: $1000-1250

Page 41: $1500-1750

Page 42: Top - $500-650
Bottom - $150-225

Page 59: $700-850

Page 60: $700-850

Page 61: Complete unit - $2000+

Page 62: $2000+

Page 63: $2000+

Page 64: $2000+

Page 65: $1900-2100

Page 66: $1900-2100

Page 67: $1300-1500

Page 68: $1700-1900

Page 69: $1000-1250

Page 70: $1000-1250

Page 71: $1200-1400

Page 72: $1000-1250

Page 73: $1200-1400

Page 74: $1200-1400

Page 75: $1200-1400

Page 76: $1200-1400

Page 77: $1800-2000

Page 78: $1800-2000

Page 79: $1800-2000

Page 80: $1800-2000

Page 81: $1800-2000

Page 82: $1800-2000

Page 83: $1500-1700

Page 84: $1800-2000

Page 85: $1800-2000

Page 86: $1800-2000

Price Guide

Page 87: $1800-2000

Page 88: $1800-2000

Page 89: $1800-2000

Page 90: $2000-2200

Page 91: $2000-2200

Page 92: $2000-2200

Page 93: $1500-1700

Page 94: $1500-1700

Page 95: Top - $800-1000
Bottom - $1300-1500

Page 96: Top left - $400-600
Top right - $500-700
Bottom - $200-250

Page 97: Top left - $125-200
Top right - $800-1000
Bottom - $600-750

Page 98: Top left - $125-200
Top right - $350-500
Bottom left - $500-700
Bottom right - $200-275

Page 102: $1000-1200

Page 103: $ 1700-2000

Page 104: Top left - $1800-2000
Top right - $1000-1200
Middle - $2300-2500
Bottom left - $1500-1700
Bottom right - $1000-1200

Page 105: $2350+

Page 106: $2350+

Page 107: $2350+

Page 108: $2350+

Page 109: Cabinet $1000-12000
Side unit $250-400

Page 110: Top - (with all units and icebox included) $4500+
Bottom main cabinet - $3500+
Bottom - (Cabinet off to the side) - $1000-1200

Page 111: Top - (with units included) - $1800-2000

Page 112: $1100-1300

Page 113: $1100-1300

Page 114: $1100-1300

Page 115: Main cabinet - $1750-2000
Side units - $250-400

Page 116: Top - $250-350
Bottom - $150-250

Page 117: Top - $400-650
Middle - $400-650
Bottom - $250-325

Page 118: Top - $600-800
Bottom (closed cupboard) $375-450

Page 119: $500-700

Page 120: Top 3 pictures - $1300-1500
Bottom - $1300-1500

Page 121: Top - $1300-1500
Bottom - $1000-1250

Page 122: $1500-1700

Page 123: $1000-1300

Page 124: $1750-2000

Page 125: Top $2300+
Bottom - $1500-1700

Page 126: Top - $1500-1700
Bottom - 2350+

Page 127: Top - $1700-1900
Bottom - $1500-1700

Page 128: Top - $1700-1900
Bottom - $1300-1500

Page 129: Top - $1500-1700
Bottom $1500-1700

Page 130: Top - 1300-1500
Bottom $1300-1500

Page 131: Top - $2000+
Bottom - $1200-1400

Page 132: $2000+